Praise for *Dinosaurs in the Cornfield*

"*Dinosaurs in the Cornfield* is a heart-warming, soul-lifting journey down the country road of childhood. Author William Hardison's descriptive prose and his ear for the Tennessee rural accent bring to life idyllic summertimes on a farm with Grandpa, a wise gentleman whose wit and wisdom not only helped his grandson to understand the world around him, but also the reader as well. Candice Smith's illustrations add extra charm to the story. *Dinosaurs in the Cornfield* is a delightful book for all ages and for all seasons of life."

— Mary W. Schaller, author of *Deliver Us from Evil: A Southern Belle in Europe at the Outbreak of World War I* (University of South Carolina Press)

"Having heard Bill speak many times, I expected a well-woven story. What I read was an enchanting memoir showing how simple lessons from Grandpa's farm could have real-world value. His vivid descriptions pull the reader into the vignettes, allowing reflection on lessons from their own childhood. Grandpa was a wise man, and I am honored to have learned some of his teachings myself."

— Susan Schwartz RN, MSN, MSHA, co-president of the Richmond chapter of the Virginia Writers Club, and anthologist of the three-volume set *Nightmares and Echoes*. Her story "Blurred Line" was nominated for a Bram Stoker Award for long fiction by the Horror Writer's Association, January 2017. www.susanschwartzauthor.com

"'Delightful and insightful'—that's what comes to mind when reading Bill Hardison's new book, *Dinosaurs in the Cornfield*. Every child should have a grandfather like Bill's—sturdy, present, and wise. I highly recommend this collection of thought-provoking life stories for readers looking for a wisdom that makes life worth living."

— Dr. Roberta Damon, marriage and family therapist, churchwoman, and author of the new book, *Dear Mrs. Noah* (Crosslink Publishing, 2017), *A Voice Beyond Weeping* (2002), and *Relationship Skills: Leadership Skills for Women* (1993)

"Who knew that the cure for my middle-aged restlessness was searching for fossils in the cornfield, taking good notes with a carpenter's pencil, or using every pot and pan in the house to catch the rain through the holey roof? Bill Hardison has given us a gift—a book I didn't want to end, and one I will read again and again. His stories come alive in the telling and remind me of what it takes to be fully alive."

— Anthony Romanello, author of *Random Thoughts: Reflections on Public Service, Fatherhood, and Middle Age*

"Dr. Hardison is a master storyteller, as evidenced in every chapter of *Dinosaurs in the Cornfield*. The life lessons and earthy wisdom woven through the enchanting and heartwarming stories of his adventures with his grandpa on the family farm in rural Tennessee are both timeless and inspirational. Each chapter will touch your heart, moving the reader to tears or genuine laughter. This is a must-read for parents and grandparents who strive to instill positive values and strength of character in the 'young'uns' they love."

— Monica L. White, Director of Student Services, Coordinator Ph.D. Program in Health Related Sciences, College of Health Professions, Virginia Commonwealth University

DINOSAURS
in
the CORNFIELD

DINOSAURS in the CORNFIELD

Lessons Unearthed on My Grandfather's Farm

by William B. Hardison, Jr.

ISBN 978-1-947860-06-3
LCCN 2018933447

Printed in the United States

Published by
Brandylane Publishers, Inc.

PUBLISHERS OF BOOKS   SINCE 1985

This book is dedicated to

Lēgie's son, my father,
Dr. W. Barker Hardison
who mastered the same rare wisdom from the farm
and inspired me to value the virtue of wisdom

to my mom, *Lois Hardison*
and my wife, *Carolyn Hardison*
for their tireless encouragement

I would like to thank Grandpa's other grandson, my brother,
Rick Hardison
who shared these adventures with me

and Grandpa's great-grandchildren,
Jonathan, Matthew, Drew, and Susan,

and his great-great-grandchildren,
Graham, Charlotte Anne, Will, and John
who will, each in their own way, carry the tradition into the future

Contents

How to Pronounce a Welch Name

Lēgie is a Welch given name, pronounced LEÉ-ghee (with long ē's). It may be derived from the Old English "liege," meaning "lord of the land."

Lēgie's mother, Mary "Mollie" Jones, was of Welch ancestry. She had eleven children, and she gave seven of them Welch names. In addition to Lēgie, there was Cordie Mai, Zuleika, Sula, Scottie, Oslin, and Alta. Those were unusual names in that remote Tennessee farming community, filled with Joes and Sams, Buds and Bills, Sues and Annies and Lauras.

According to US census records, as of 2010, there was only one man in America who had the first name Lēgie.

"Grandpa"
Age 61
6'4" / 230 lbs.

Billy
Age 6
3'10" / 40 lbs.

How the "Grandpa Stories" Came to Be:
An Introduction

*"You have to do your own growing up,
no matter how tall your grandfather was."*
—Abraham Lincoln

It was midnight on a Saturday in September of 1971. I was at home in my upstairs office, sitting at my desk beneath the glow of a single lamp. A freshly sharpened #2 pencil prodded me with a pungent smell of wood as it lay untouched before me on a yellow pad. The pencil was shouting at me. *I can't do this by myself!* it said. But my mind was as blank as the pad.

I was twenty-seven, a young pastor facing another 11:00 a.m. Sunday deadline. In a few short hours, I would be expected to stand behind a pulpit and deliver. It was officially time to panic.

In that moment, a memory so old that it felt as if it came from another lifetime began to materialize, and I recalled a family visit to my grandparents' farm in Tennessee. I was seven years old, and my brother Rick was three. One evening, as we began settling down for the night, a fierce storm struck. In my imagination, I could see the shadows from the fireplace flickering with a fury on the faded wallpaper as the winds blew outside. I could smell the smoke as the wood spat and crackled. Reliving the memory of the storm, I realized that it told a vivid story about fear and laughter, faith and courage.

As I came to myself, sitting safely at my desk, it dawned on me that I might be able to build a sermon around the story. The tale of the monster storm had everything my sermon needed:

drama, humor, and color. Sharing it would be easy. My memory of that night was so vivid, I could recall every detail as clearly as if it had happened yesterday. And for reasons I didn't understand, it seemed as if the story itself was begging to be told.

I took up my pencil and scribbled an outline of my sermon on the yellow pad as quickly as I could, careful not to leave out any detail. I rehearsed it briefly in my mind, then settled into bed and closed my eyes to wait for whatever the coming day would bring.

Sunday morning came quickly. As the clock struck eleven, I stood nervously behind the pulpit and began my homily. First, I read from Isaiah, describing God's word as being like the rain that falls to the earth, always fulfilling its purpose. I described how God's blessings also fall on us, soaking us to the bone.

As I spoke, I could tell that the sermon was unfolding too slowly. The congregants were fidgeting, punctuating my narrative with well-placed yawns. I knew I was losing them. I decided to skip a couple of points and hurry on. Maybe the story from the farm would capture them.

I began to describe the scene in the farmhouse—and suddenly, the congregation seemed riveted to every detail. They leaned forward in the pews, completely focused, drinking in my story like thirsty pilgrims at an oasis.

Afterward, I was surprised when a dozen people came up to me, wanting to know more about my grandfather. They said things like, "I loved your story. Your description of the crackling fire in the old stone fireplace really took me back to my childhood." Some asked, "When are you going to tell more stories about your grandpa?" And one lamented, "I never knew my grandfather; can I borrow yours?" I had touched a nerve.

Over the years, responses like these were often repeated. People began calling my anecdotes about my grandfather's life on the farm "Grandpa Stories," and asking me to write them down.

In November of 2012, I went on retreat to Princeton, New Jersey to begin writing these stories that seem to have touched so many. I sat for hours in the deep recesses of Firestone Library, as story after story came rushing back to my memory. As I began to write, I discovered an unexpected bonus: from each story, a life lesson began to emerge, as if, from each experience, Grandpa had unearthed a gem from among the boulder fields that littered the farm and showed it to me, sharing his wisdom. The stories that I thought I knew so well surprised me by speaking to my adult heart. They were more than random stories—they reminded me of who my grandfather had been to me, and the legacy he had left me.

My stories had been speaking to others for decades. At last, they were speaking to me.

The "Grandpa Stories" are meant to be read as "legacy stories": as you read them, you may rediscover something of your own story that you had forgotten—perhaps something that was meant to be part of your own legacy.

After one storytelling session, a young mother with toddler in tow came to me and said, "As you were telling your story, I was reminded of how patiently my grandmother kept her gardens. I could picture her house, and almost smell the potted flowers on the front porch. I even remembered how the gravel would crunch as I walked out back in her garden among her flowers. It was all so vivid, so real. I had forgotten. You know, perhaps she was trying to teach me patience."

On another occasion, a young man told me, "You know, after years watching my grandfather sit in his easy chair with his pipe, reflecting on some problem, and seeing him resist making 'mountains out of molehills,' I've learned not to take life so seriously."

These examples illustrate how people may hear their own legacy stories while listening to my "Grandpa Stories" from down on the farm. Through my listeners' responses, I came to realize that many of us need to revisit our childhood memories, find our mentors, and sit once again at their feet.

"But," you might say, "I grew up in the city. I'm not a farmer. How can your grandfather's stories possibly apply to me?" That's a fair question. It's true that many lessons learned on the farm can be hard to replicate in an urban or suburban setting. But I have discovered that the truths found in these lessons are common to everyone's childhood, whether you grew up on a remote, rock-strewn farm in Tennessee or on the streets of Hoboken, New Jersey. In the end, it doesn't matter what life work we have been given to do. We may be businessmen and businesswomen, nurses and doctors, teachers and firemen, caregivers in homes for the aging, "butchers, bakers, and candlestick-makers." But as my grandpa used to say, "You need t' be plantin' in the fields you've been given t' plow." Scratch the surface of any cubicle in any high-rise office building in the world, and we are all just farmers, hoes in hand, planting the fields we've been given to plow.

It may be best if you just sit back, enjoy these lighthearted stories, and see what comes. You might be surprised when one of my grandpa's sayings sneaks up on you, rises up on its hind feet, looks you straight in the eye, and speaks right to your heart.

Welcome to the wonder-filled world of a lovable Tennessee dirt-farmer, a wise old country mystic in bib overalls—my grandfather, Lēgie.

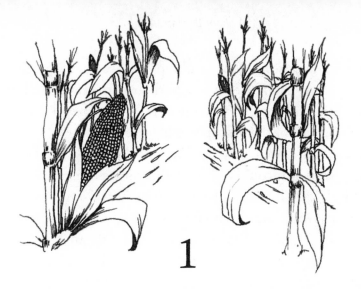

1

The Long-Lost and Finally Found Fossil

Wisdom from the Farm:

You don't have t' always be leavin' home and travelin' the world t' find excitement or t' go adventurin'. The greatest adventures and the deepest mysteries can be found right where you are, right under yer feet. You just have t' dig fer 'um.

From the front step of my childhood home in suburban Washington, DC, it was exactly 701 miles to the wooden gate that opened onto the old farm in a place called Rock Spring in Maury County, Tennessee—population: 65. As a child, always impatient to get where I was going, I knew every winding mile of the journey.

I dreaded every visit to the farm. Nothing much ever happened there, and what did happen never seemed to have much importance in the world beyond the farm's barbed-wire boundaries. The Governor didn't send photographers to take pictures of Grandma's prize-winning morning glories to frame and hang in the executive mansion. The university didn't send scientists to study the ecology of Grandpa's cedar stands. The

Nashville Tennessean didn't send reporters to cover the birth of the new calf—and if there was a pothole in the road, the county didn't even send out a crew to repair it. You had to get the shovel out of the back of the pickup and fix it yourself.

No doubt about it: Grandma and Grandpa lived off the beaten path. You could tell from the names of nearby villages like Fly, Tie Whop, and Lickskillet, where Grandma taught school in a one-room schoolhouse, that Rock Spring was a hidden-away place. The area was so remote that folks who had lived there all their lives sometimes couldn't find their way home.

Coming from the city, I found the sudden adjustment to farm living to be a challenge. Visiting Grandpa and Grandma meant leaving behind everything that summer in the city had to offer. On the farm there were no movie theaters, swimming pools, bowling alleys, radios, or telephones. Worst of all, there was no Little League baseball. I was finally six—old enough to play for the first time—but there was no Little League in Rock Spring.

We arrived at the farm late on a Tuesday afternoon the first week in July, and arriving was always a shock to the senses. The water was pure and the air was clean, but the land had a strange odor. It smelled of pine and cedar mixed with the damp scent of old rotting timbers, mud, and manure, all infused with the smell of cut hay. It was a sharp, pungent aroma, and it stank! Upon opening the car door, I wondered why they called it "fresh" air. But I found that if I breathed it long enough, the odor mysteriously went away.

We were hot and tired from our trip, and just in time for dinner. Too hungry to complain about the heat in the kitchen, we sat down to a feast: Grandma's specialty, chicken 'n' dumplin's. We went to bed early that night, without any sheets over us, trying to acclimate ourselves to the heat. After an hour or two, the evening air cooled, we pulled the sheets up around our chins and slept in peace.

The next morning, the old rooster woke me at the crack of dawn. I found Grandma in the kitchen at the back of the old farmhouse, preparing breakfast. Every morning, Grandma served fresh eggs from the henhouse; hot biscuits with hand-churned butter, gravy, bacon, and sausage; and if you had a taste for it, whole milk straight from the pail. No doubt about it: if you slept through Grandma's breakfast, you missed the best meal of the day.

Grandma always wore a flowered apron. She had one for every occasion: one for the kitchen, to hold the hot biscuits; another for the outdoors, when she fed the chickens; and another for picking apples in the orchard. She wore an apron everywhere, except when she went to Meeting down at the church.

Grandma was small compared to Grandpa, maybe 5'4". She couldn't have weighed more than one hundred pounds, but she had more energy in every pound than I did in my whole body. Despite her slight size, she could split wood in the hot sun and tote it in to keep the iron stove hot; and if you challenged her, she'd sit down at the kitchen table and arm wrestle any opponent.

Her hair had turned gray, and she kept it tied up in a bun behind her head. Her face was full of wrinkles going in every direction like roads on a roadmap, so that it looked as if it had been wadded up and pushed to the back of a drawer overnight. Every morning, she'd open the drawer, and it would come out more wrinkled than the day before. But in spite of her deeply weathered face, she had the greatest smile.

After breakfast, Grandma cleared the dishes off the kitchen table, and I began looking for something to do.

"Grandma, I'm bored," I said.

She fixed me with a stare. "Bored already, are you? Imagine that. And you just got here. Young'un, with a mind like yers, you ought never be bored. You ought t' be able t' think up somethin' t' do all on yer own. So, while yer thinker's thinkin' up somethin', you can sit over there and snap green beans into that there bowl." She pointed toward the kitchen table. "When you're finished with that, and while you're thinkin' up somethin' else t' do, you can come out back and help me carry in more firewood fer the stove; and when you finish that, you can go find yer grandpa. He'll give you somethin' t' do."

As I sat down to snap the beans, Grandma hit me with one of her smiles. All the wrinkles instantly disappeared right off her face, and it was as if the sun had come out. It was miraculous. Then, right after laying that amazing smile on me, she turned and went out the screen door onto the back porch to do the washing, leaving me to snap the beans alone.

I frowned. I should have known that if I told Grandma I was bored, she'd rattle off a list of chores to keep me busy. But I was looking for something exciting to do—something less like work, and more like fun. Besides, snapping beans was something that was meant to be done while you were talking to somebody. I'd never seen anybody snap beans alone. So, leaving the beans for someone else to snap, I ran outside to ask her where I could find Grandpa.

I pushed the screen door out of my way as I ran out onto the back porch, forgetting one of Grandma's house rules. The spring that was attached to the screen door recoiled, and the door slammed behind me with a wooden clap—loud, like when Grandpa fired his rifle. When the door whacked the jam, it startled the chickens, and they took off on short, frantic flights, screeching, squawking, and scattering dust and feathers in every direction.

The screen door incident had happened before, and Grandma said that the slamming of the door was such a fright to the hens that they wouldn't lay their eggs for days. She turned and looked at me over top of her granny glasses, which were resting half way down her nose. "Billy, how many times do I have t' tell you not t' slam the screen door?

"Sorry, Grandma. I forgot."

"Well, we need t' work on yer rememberin'," she mumbled. Grandma had such a good nature that she'd never use an angry tone of voice, but she was a pretty good mumbler.

After the chickens had come back to earth and calmed themselves down, Grandma went back to her washing. She had a scrub board sitting in a large tub of sudsy hot water. She scrubbed the clothes on the board, she rinsed them, and wrung them out by hand. Then she hung them on a line to dry in the bright sunshine.

"Grandma, I'm tired of snapping beans."

"Someone's gotta snap those beans, Billy. Finish yer chores first. Then I'll tell you where you can find yer grandpa."

I went back into the kitchen and snapped the beans in record time. When I went outside to tell Grandma that I'd finished, she smiled that smile and said, "Yer grandpa's down at the barn, buildin' a new trough fer sloppin' the hogs. He said that he has somethin' interestin' he's been wantin' t' show you."

I turned and hurried back across the porch and through the screen door, catching it on the inside so that it wouldn't slam behind me. Then I ran through the house and out the front door, and started down the big hill toward the barn, which sat almost a quarter of a mile away at the bottom of the barren hillside, one hundred and fifty feet below the farmhouse. There were no trees or bushes or boulders on that hill, just hard-packed earth strewn with millions of loose pebbles, and it was easy to lose your footing if you were in a hurry.

About halfway down the hill, I spotted Grandpa in front of the barn. He was using a big rubber mallet to pound out dents in a metal trough.

"Hey, Grandpa!" I shouted. "I'm coming!"

Suddenly, my sneakers went flying out from under me, and I landed on my backside and slid about three or four feet down the hill, scraping a red burn on the palms of my hands and the backs of my legs.

Grandpa had probably known I was going to fall before I even left the house, but he didn't even turn around to see what damage I'd done. He just kept right on working. No words of comfort. No coming up the hill to pick me up and dust me off. That was Grandpa's way. I guess he figured that if a man got himself into some small jam on account of not being too smart, it was sometimes best to leave him alone and make him get up by himself.

When Grandpa didn't come to help me, and I had to tend to myself, it made me feel bigger than if he had come running up the hill to see if I was okay. So I picked myself up, looked at my scraped hands, dusted the dirt off my legs, and walked the rest of the way down to where Grandpa was working.

The July morning was hot and humid, but whatever the weather, Grandpa always wore long-sleeved shirts that never quite reached his wrists. His long arms protruded out of his sleeves and ended in huge hands gnarled from years of stretching barbed-wire fencing, tending to farm animals, logging trees, and wrestling with mule-drawn plows to break up the rocky soil. Most days, he wore Duck Head blue denim overalls covered with pockets, in which he carried a pair of scissors, a pair of work gloves, a pocketknife, a loop of string, a big handkerchief, a pair of small pliers, and any small tools he thought he might need for the day.

Grandpa didn't stop to acknowledge me when I arrived. He was completely absorbed in finishing the trough. So I interrupted him.

"Grandpa, I'm bored," I said, checking out my injured elbow.

"Bored, are you?"

He put one hand on his back, straightened himself to his full height, and took a long look at me. When Grandpa was standing tall, it amazed me how big a man he was. His forbearers had been timbermen of enormous strength and stature who made their living harvesting the evergreen forests on the granite hillsides of Maine, and like them, he was a giant, rawboned and grizzled. His prodigious strength was legendary; he was said to be the strongest man in the county. He could wrestle a contrary heifer to the ground, or lift a two-hundred-pound sow shoulder-high and place her squirming into the back of his battered old Chevy pickup.

At sixty-one years old, Grandpa stood 6'4" and weighed 230 pounds. By comparison, I was six years old, weighed in right at forty pounds, and stood 3'10". I was small for my age, and Grandpa loomed over me. If he hadn't had such a gentle nature, he would have been intimidating. In fact, the summer before, when I was just five, I had seen Grandpa corner a skittish young goat that had gotten inside the farmyard and was disturbing the guinea fowl. Grandpa pinned the kid against the wire fence that enclosed the farmyard. Then he picked up the squirming animal and held it firmly under his left arm. The kid was shaking with fear—but then Grandpa whispered in its ear, and suddenly, it stopped shaking and went completely quiet, yielding itself to Grandpa's strength.

I always wondered what Grandpa said to the animals. They'd follow him anywhere.

On this occasion, he looked down at me and said, "Billy, grab yer walkin' stick and come with me. I've got somethin' t' show you."

So we fetched our walking sticks, which were leaning against the side of the barn and set off for the lower forty, a quarter-mile to the south.

The lower forty was an odd sort of place. It was the lowest land on the farm—so low that it was swampy in areas where the creek flowed alongside the Rock Spring Road and formed its eastern boundary. The road had been built up, so that it stood two feet or more above the field. That way, the shoulder wouldn't give way as easily if the creek rose and flooded the area.

There were forty acres of land in that field, which was why it was called the "lower forty." Grandpa sometimes used it for pasturing the cows, but I always thought the cows that grazed there came back to the barn in the evening with puzzled looks on their faces. They'd find a tuft of wild grass here and there, but it was mostly flat land, littered with huge, table-topped limestone slabs rising a foot or two off the ground. Each slab was ten or twelve yards across, and they were everywhere. They were colored all shades of gray, with patches of green moss growing in the cracks and crevices. You could tell that those boulders were really old, older than regular rocks. They even smelled old—moldy and damp.

I wasn't surprised that the cows looked confused when they came back from the lower forty. Even they knew grazing wasn't supposed to be that hard. Faced with a field strewn with boulders, most farmers would have given up and moved west to richer, tillable soils, but Grandpa wasn't intimidated. He had fortitude like his New England forbearers. He was a "stay-putter."

We were walking through the boulder field when Grandpa stopped at one of the tabletop outcroppings. "Billy," he said, "stand back, right over there." He pointed. He wanted me out of the way in case something was to break loose unexpectedly. "Now watch."

Grandpa wedged his walking stick into a crack near the top of one of the flat-topped boulders. Then, as he pressed down with all his weight, up popped a piece of rock about the shape and size of a dinner plate. It went clattering off across the tabletop, falling harmlessly into the wild grass.

I'd never seen anything like it. I stepped closer and squatted down on my haunches, balancing myself on the balls of my red Keds sneakers, and leaned forward, afraid to touch it. When I looked closely, I saw a strange image pressed down into the rock like an ancient fingerprint. Ten inches long, oval, with ribs coming off a spine that ran down the middle, it looked like something that might once have been alive.

"Is that a fossil, Grandpa?"

"Yep, it'd be a fossil, alright."

"Looks like a leaf," I said, eyeballing the find up close.

"Nope. It'd be an old fish."

I twisted around, shielding my eyes against the glare of the sun, and looked up at him. "How old?" I said.

"Old is old," he said. Grandpa wasn't given to using too many words. Getting a lot of words out of Grandpa was like trying to squeeze raisins to make grape juice.

I was astonished. It was such an unexpected find, and in such an unlikely place! Who would have thought that the fossil of a prehistoric fish would be unearthed on a remote, boulder-strewn farm in the middle of Tennessee, hundreds of miles from the nearest ocean? I couldn't get over it.

"How'd it get here?"

"Don't know. You'll have t' ask yer pa. He found fossils like this one when he was yer age."

I made a mental note to ask my dad about the fossil as soon as we got back to the farmhouse for lunch. Then, bending closer so that I was looking straight down at the smallish fossil, I said, "Grandpa, how did you know there'd be a fossil under this rock?"

"Oh, they'd be all over the place," he said. From his tone, he seemed a little afraid that he'd gotten something started up in me that he wasn't likely to hear the end of anytime soon.

"Have you found any other kinds of fossils?"

"Heard tell of a young boy 'bout yer age up toward Franklin, fifteen miles north from here." He pointed up the road to show me the way. "Word is that he found a big bone. Turned out t' be some sorta elephant."

"How big?" I asked.

"Don't rightly know. Big is big!"

"That would have to be a mammoth—or a mastodon," I said, trying to remember from the picture books at school which one looked more like a big elephant.

"Could be," he said.

"Any others?"

"Well, there'd be an ancient kinda turtle, ugly-lookin' thing, that still lives in the mud at the bottom of the Duck River 'bout a mile south." Hat in hand, he pointed toward the river. "Some say it'd be prehistoric."

As I knelt there, listening to Grandpa's words, my imagination flamed up like the struck head of a matchstick. By the light of that flame, I saw buffalo roaming in the tall grass beyond the upper forty, woolly mammoths with long curved tusks slowly moving along the ridgeline southwest of the farmhouse in search of a salt lick, and huge prehistoric creatures with long necks trying to hide in the tall corn. Dinosaurs! We'd studied them in school. "Really, Grandpa? Can we go see?"

"Nope! We got work t' do. Can't go 'round spendin' all yer time adventurin' when there's farmin' needs doin'."

I examined the fossil in silence. Finally, Grandpa said, "If'n you put yer ear down and listen t' it real close, it'll speak t' you."

Grandpa had to be playing some sort of game with me. I was only six, but I knew some grown-ups would play tricks on you when you were that age. "Grandpa, fossils can't talk to you. They've been dead for a million years, maybe more."

"Sure of that, are you?"

"Yeah, I'm sure."

"Maybe so, maybe no," he said.

I got down on both knees and put my ear close to the fossil, listening.

"The fossil isn't saying anything, Grandpa."

"That'd be strange," he said. "It talked t' me."

I wasn't convinced, but Grandpa didn't say anything more. "Okay, Grandpa. What did the fossil say?"

"The fossil said, 'Don't ever be surprised when you find dinosaurs in yer cornfield.'"

"What's that supposed to mean?" I asked.

"It was tryin' t' say that if'n you pay close attention, you can find the most unlikely things in the most familiar places."

"And what's that supposed to mean?" I said.

"Means you don't have t' go traipsin' all over the place tryin' t' find amazin' things. You don't have t' travel t' faraway places like Memphis t' see the Mississippi River, or go into the caverns up in Kentucky t' see the wonders of Mother Nature, 'cause the most amazin' things you can imagine are happenin' right under yer feet where you've been standin' all the time. So there'd be no reason fer you t' ever be bored on the farm, 'cause all the really excitin' things—the things that matter—happen right at home, if'n you keep yer eyes sharp and listen real close."

"Okay, Grandpa. Tell me another ordinary thing about the farm that's actually interesting," I said.

"Billy, if'n you know where t' look, every ordinary thing has somethin' extraordinary hidden inside. Take the farmhouse, fer example."

"The farmhouse?"

"Yep! That old house probably doesn't seem like much t' you, with its drafts lurkin' in the corners, its splintered floorboards, and the dirt daubers comin' through the holes in the window screens and buildin' their nests in the corners of the ceilin'. The linoleum's cracked and worn clean through in places, and some boards on the back porch are close t' rottin' and need replacin'."

"It's okay, Grandpa," I said—not wanting him to feel too bad about the house.

"It'd be more'n okay," he said. "If'n you were t' notice the old place real close, tryin' t' find somethin' excitin', you'd be in fer a real surprise."

"Like what, Grandpa?"

"Well, right there underneath yer feet, and behind the wallboards, you'd find old logs holdin' up the whole house. There are parts of that farmhouse that were built over a hundred years ago, by some of the first settlers comin' through this region. You wouldn't know it, 'cause you haven't been practicin' yer noticin', but Billy, you're actually livin' in a log cabin, just like young'uns yer age did when there were still wild boars and bears and Indians in the woods."

"No kidding, Grandpa; really?!"

He nodded at me. "Billy, if'n you really go t' noticin' the ordinary things all 'round you, you're likely gonna find excitin' things that are so wondrous, you'll never be bored again."

I was amazed. First, I had discovered that there were dinosaurs hiding in Grandpa's cornfields, lumbering through the trees up on the ridgeline and stalking prey among the rocks in the boulder fields. Now, Grandpa was telling me that we were living in an old log cabin. Suddenly, the farm and the farmhouse were full of vivid new sights and sounds. I imagined buckskin jackets hanging on pegs behind the doors, and flintlock rifles standing in the corners. I heard covered wagons rumbling down ancient roadways cut through the primitive forest, and saw bearskin pelts hanging from the beams in the ceiling, waiting to be rafted down the river to the nearest fur-trading post. The whole farm was coming alive for me.

"Grandpa, show me the logs!"

"Later," he said, "The logs've been there fer a hundred years. They'll be there fer another day or two. I 'spect it'd be 'bout time fer lunch."

Grandpa glanced up toward the farmhouse in the distance, and I did too. I spotted Grandma out on the porch with her hands on her hips, looking down toward the barn. "Best be gettin' home," Grandpa said. "Grandma's expectin' us."

I set off running as fast as I could, leaving Grandpa behind. I couldn't wait to tell Grandma that we had found a real fossil!

It was a long run, and I was really gassed by the time I got up the hill. I jumped the steps two at a time, carefully closed the screen door behind me, and ran into the kitchen.

"Grandma, Grandma! Guess what?"

"What, Billy?" she said, busily setting lunch fixings on the kitchen table.

Every time Grandma called me Billy, I cringed. My mom and dad always called me "Bill," but Grandma and Grandpa called me "Billy," and that made me feel small. Whenever Grandma called me "Billy," I was reminded that I was real skinny for my age. I liked "Bill" much better, but to Grandma and Grandpa, I was always "Billy." I lived with it as best I could.

"Grandpa and I found the fossil of an old fish in a rock down in the lower forty."

"Did, did you? How about that." She didn't seem too surprised.

At that moment, Dad came into the kitchen for lunch, and I heard Grandpa arrive at the back porch, banging his boots on the edge of the steps to knock the mud loose. Grandma was pouring cool spring water into our glasses. That water tasted so good after we'd been out in the heat. After a couple of swallows, I could breathe again.

"Dad, guess what?"

"What?"

"Grandpa and I found a fossil of an old fish down in the lower forty."

"You did? That's interesting. You know, when I was a boy growing up on the farm, I found fossils all over the place."

"I asked Grandpa how the fish fossil came to be here on the farm, and he said to ask you. So, Dad, how'd the fossil get to be on the farm?"

"There'll be time for that story later," he said. It was clear from his tone that lunch would come first.

Everyone sat down, and after thanking the Good Lord for our food, we ate fried chicken with potato salad, tomatoes fresh off the vine, and the beans I'd snapped earlier that morning.

After polishing off lunch with a sweet cup of vanilla custard, we all got up from the table. Before we left the kitchen, I caught Dad and said, "Dad, can we go down to the boulders? I'll show you the fossil we found."

Mom spoke up. "Bill, the sun gets too hot in the afternoon to go out into the fields. We all need to take a rest until it cools off some. Maybe this evening."

"Best mind yer mom," Grandma said. "Your fossil's not goin' anywhere between now and then. We've got 'Dinner on the Grounds' coming up after Meetin' this Sunday, and I need to bake some apple pies." She looked straight at me and said, "I reckon I'm gonna need some help pickin' the apples."

I didn't say anything. I had enough chores to do without volunteering to pick apples.

Dad said, "Tell you what, son. Maybe before supper I'll tell you a story about the fossil you found."

"Okay, Dad," I said disappointed that no one seemed as excited about the find as I was. "Right before supper; you promise?"

He promised.

Through all this, Grandpa sat at the table, eating, and didn't say a thing. As far back as I could remember, Grandpa had never said anything at meals. When it came to eating, he was all business.

After lunch, I went into the bedroom, lay down on my bed, and tried to rest—but I couldn't sleep. I was still thinking about the fish fossil. For millions of years, it had been lost inside that big boulder; but today, after all those years trapped in the dark, it had finally been found. And while I lay there, trying to stay cool, I imagined herds of wild buffalo making their way north along what would become the Natchez Trace, passing just west of the farm. I saw giant ground sloths that lived beyond the old forest grazing in the grasslands up behind the farmhouse, and flying pterodactyls diving into the small lake beyond Grandma's garden. I even saw huge raptors, running dinosaurs with sharp teeth, hiding in Grandpa's woods.

I decided to read a couple of comic books to pass the time and get the dinosaurs off my mind. Finally, around four o'clock, Dad came to get me and said, "You still want to hear the story about the fossil?"

"Yeah, Dad, I've been waiting all afternoon."

"Come out on the porch. We'll rock in the rocking chairs, and I'll tell you everything I know."

I jumped out of bed, leaving the comic books open on the mattress. There was a nice breeze on the porch, and it carried away some of the leftover heat from the day. It was good storytelling weather.

After we got to rocking, Dad said, "Okay. What do you want to know?"

I said, "If there was a fish, then there had to have been a pond or a lake where it lived, right?"

"Right," he said. "But your fish had a much bigger home than a lake."

"How much bigger?"

"Well," he said, "three hundred and fifty million years ago, this whole region of Middle Tennessee, including our farm, all of Maury County, and the land all the way up to Nashville and down into Alabama, was covered by a huge inland sea. That sea was full of fish of every description, including ancient sharks and huge prehistoric sturgeon-like fish, and many others."

"Really?"

"Really," he said. "This whole farm was deep underwater. That sea was eighty miles wide and a hundred miles long. Big duckbilled creatures called hadrosaurs waded in its shallows, hunting for food. The hadrosaur was one of the oldest of the walking dinosaurs, and fossil hunters have found their remains up on the West Highland Rim that marks the western edge of the sea, about twenty-five miles that way." He pointed to the west. "Over millions of years, the skeletons of these ancient creatures, which were full of calcium, fell to the bottom; and under great pressure from the seawater above, they were compressed into limestone rock. Those flat-topped boulders where you and Grandpa found the fossil this morning are solid limestone."

"So where'd all the water go?" I said.

"That's a good question. Eventually, the seabed began to rise and form what's called the Nashville Dome. As the land rose, all the seawater drained off, and there's a theory that the drainage formed great rivers like the Cumberland, the Tennessee, and the Duck Rivers. As the sea bottom rose to the surface, it exposed hundreds of table-topped limestone outcroppings like the ones you see down in the lower forty."

Dad and I talked for most of thirty minutes about my fossil. He told me about the fossils he'd found on the farm when he was a boy my age—mostly small sea animals called trilobites.

"Dad, draw me a picture of a trilobite." I wanted to see a picture in case I found one while I was on one of the fossil-hunting expeditions I was planning. Maybe if I could get out of apple-picking, I'd go the next morning.

He obliged me. Just as he finished my drawing, Grandma came to the screen door to tell us that supper was on the table: chicken 'n' dumplin's, yellow squash, country biscuits with honey left over from breakfast, snap beans left over from lunch, and fresh apple pie for dessert. Grandma was already practicing for tomorrow's baking.

While the rest of us cleaned up the kitchen, Grandpa went down to check on the sheep and see that they were gathered safely into the sheep pens for the night. He milked the cows, and when he was finished, he went and sat on the front porch to enjoy the last two hours of sunlight.

After my brother Rick and I had our baths, we joined the others on the front porch. The grown-ups were swapping stories and listening to news, mixed generously with rumor, of what was happening on neighboring farms or in the lives of relatives scattered around the countryside. We sat in cane-bottom rocking chairs and swings with chains bolted into the beams above the porch, and watched the sunlight fade behind the cedar trees in the distance, way off across the road five hundred yards from the house.

So there it was: a hot day in July, the first day I ever listened to a fossil. Or rather, to be precise, the fossil had talked to Grandpa; and then Grandpa had explained to me what it said. Maybe the reason the fossil hadn't talked to me was because it thought that since I was only six years old, I was too dumb to talk to. Between my feet going out from under me or my sliding four feet down the hill on my rump, and not being able to hear the fossil speak, I didn't feel like too smart a fella. I didn't do these things on purpose, but somehow they happened to me all the time. Maybe one day, I thought, I'll grow up big and wise as Grandpa and be able to hear what fossils have to say. I hoped so, 'cause fossils seemed to have a lot of wise things to teach me.

And as it turned out, the fossil was right. In the very place where I thought nothing much ever happened, the most important events of my young life were taking place, and I was too young to know it. Looking back fifty years later, there's an ache in me that wishes I could go back and do the "nothing" all over again. It wasn't until I was an adult that I realized the many ways that the wisdom from the farm had shaped my life for the better.

Now, It's Your Turn:

If anything in my story or in Grandpa's "Wisdom from the Farm" reminds you of something in your story, you might want to make a note of it here. If you want to interactively engage with Dinosaurs in the Cornfield, pause a moment at the end of each chapter to record a childhood memory that may have come to mind. After you finish the book, you can gather up all your notes, and when you do, they might speak to you in ways you weren't expecting.

_____

_____

_____

_____

_____

_____

_____

_____

_____

_____

_____

_____

_____

_____

_____

_____

_____

_____

_____

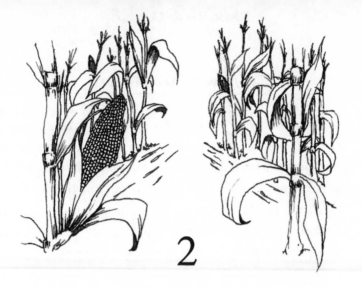

2

What 'Olde' Things Have to Say

Wisdom from the Farm:

No matter where you are, Olde has been there before you, and Olde knows how things came t' be. Olde is always workin' behind the scenes, even when you're not aware of it. New is always standin' on the shoulders of Olde, so you oughtta always be listenin' t' what Olde has t' say, 'cause Olde is usually wiser than New.

I dreamed about fossils that night. When Thursday morning dawned, I was all set to go fossil hunting. I was obsessed with dinosaurs, and couldn't think about anything else.

After breakfast, I found Grandpa sitting on the step of the back porch, using a long nail to pick burrs and small stones out of the soles of his boots.

"Grandpa, can we go fossil hunting today?"

"Nope!" he said. That was it—just "nope." He didn't need to explain himself to a child. He was tending to grown-up business.

Grandpa finished picking the burrs from his shoes and stood up. As he left the porch and passed through the orchard behind the house, where Grandma was gathering apples, I tagged along after him. "Where are you going, Grandpa?"

"Gonna walk over the hill t' the Scott farm t' see Daisy."

"Who's Daisy?"

"Daisy's one of Mr. Scott's milk cows. She's sick."

"What's she sick with?"

"Don't rightly know 'til I see her."

"Can I come?"

"Nope," he said again. "Grandma needs you here t' help with the apple-pickin'."

Picking apples with Grandma didn't mean putting a ladder up in a tree and climbing up to pluck ripe, red, sweet apples off the limb. Grandma's version of "picking apples" meant grabbing half-rotten, sour green apples up off the ground where they'd already fallen. Using her apron as a makeshift bucket, Grandma would bend to collect the apples, until she'd gathered a couple dozen or so. Then she would unload them into a pail. These weren't "eating" apples—Grandma's apples were for cooking, for fried apples and apple pies and apple jellies with a whole lot of sugar added to cover up the sourness.

I liked Grandma's apple pie just fine, but picking apples couldn't be nearly as much fun as seeing Grandpa whisper into the ear of a sick animal and watching it begin to get well. I'd never seen him tend to a sick animal before, but I'd heard some amazing stories. Grandpa was the unofficial local vet, and all the farmers trusted him with the care of their animals.

I wanted to keep following Grandpa; but Grandma, who was already at work in the orchard, must have heard our conversation. As we passed her, she turned her head toward me from her bent-over position and said, "Billy, come over here. Bring that small pail, and help me pick these apples."

Grandpa continued over the hill toward the Scott farm, and I reluctantly stopped to help Grandma. I approached her carefully: sometimes, while picking apples with Grandma, you'd reach for an apple with a brownish, bruised spot on it, and a yellow jacket would've beaten you to it. I could see them now, flying lazily around her.

"Grandma, one of those yellow jackets is gonna sting me."

"Don't you worry none 'bout the yellow jackets. They won't bother you if'n you don't bother them." That was just the kind of thing grown-ups said right before you got stung. But I decided to trust her, and picked up the pail.

Using my thumb and one finger like a pincer, I slowly lifted the first apple. There was a yellow jacket on the underside, so I set it back down real carefully.

The next apple had a big bruise on the underside. I bent over as far as I could to inspect the entire surface and, not seeing any yellow jacket, used my pincer method to pick it up. I examined it cautiously, and put it in the pail.

I was getting the hang of picking apples. If I bent over far enough, I found I could practically see the whole apple before I touched it.

About thirty minutes later, I had almost filled my pail when Grandpa came walking back over the hill, just in time for lunch. We all went inside for chicken salad sandwiches made with the biscuits left over from breakfast, celery sticks, applesauce, and fresh water from the well. At the table, I asked Grandpa how Daisy was doing.

"Aw, she'll be okay in a day or two."

"What's wrong with her?" I asked.

"I'm thinkin' it'd probably just be the colic. Colic can make a cow real sick. Found her flat on her side, unable t' get up on her feet, and breathin' heavy. But she just needed some Epsom salts and someone t' keep her hydrated real good. Mr. Scott just opened up a new pasture, and Daisy probably overgrazed."

Then Grandpa changed the subject. "Billy, I need t' go into town this afternoon t' the co-op. I need some fertilizer and feed fer the animals. Yer Grandma needs help hangin' out the wash, and sweepin' the house. You can stay here, or you can ride into town with me."

No contest, I thought. I'd rather go to town with Grandpa any day. Everywhere you went with Grandpa, you'd find yourself swept up in some unexpected adventure.

"I'll ride with you, Grandpa."

"Okay then, get movin'. We'd best be gettin' on our way."

Grandma didn't seem to object to my going with Grandpa. She even slipped a one-dollar bill into my pocket as I started down the porch steps toward the truck. Grandma knew there might be something in town I'd want to buy, like the latest comic books, and Grandpa might not be so generous. He wasn't real keen on my reading so many comic books.

"Gee, thanks, Grandma," I said, and was off down the steps two at a time. I crossed the yard running, got one foot on the truck's running board, and was into my seat before Grandpa could even crank the starter.

Grandpa had an old Chevy pickup truck that, in its glory days, might have been a bright forest green. Nobody knew how old the battered pickup was, but it was old enough that the hot Middle Tennessee sun had faded the paint to a dull blue-gray version of the green it had once been.

"Grandpa, how old is this truck?"

"Don't exactly know," he said. "It'd be the first truck I ever owned. Always used the horses and wagon before. Bought it used, and never thought t' ask the fella how old it was. Why d'you want t' know?"

"I was just wondering if this old truck was a sort of fossil."

"Nope!" he said. "It's old, but it isn't a fossil."

The age of the truck didn't seem to matter one bit to Grandpa, though considering how broken-down it was, I thought it might be time for him to buy a new one. The paint job wasn't the only thing wearing thin. The rubber on the clutch pedal had worn off from years of shifting gears, and the brake pedal was worn down to shiny metal from when Grandpa had brought the old truck to many a sudden stop trying to avoid a stray cow or sheep standing in the middle of the road. When I got in, I had to slam the door shut real hard, and it made a metal clunk as it closed, which always left me wondering whether it might just fly open rounding the next bend. The floorboard was rusted clean through in spots, so I could see the crushed rock roadway passing by fast beneath my feet. Neither the driver's nor the passenger's side windows would roll up, so when we came to a stop, the dust that we'd been leaving behind caught up to us and filled the cab, covering everything from the dashboard to the seats. Yep—every trip to town was an adventure.

Grandpa always sat up real straight in the seat when he drove. He was so tall that his balding head almost touched the top of the cab, and tapped against it every time we hit a bump in the road. It was kind of funny watching him. He drove like a teenager on his first time behind the wheel, being real careful, not wanting to make a mistake.

We headed south down the old Rock Spring Road, which passed right by the farm. After a mile, we turned right at the Rock Springs Baptist Church and headed west toward town on Sowell Mill Pike.

Unlike many of the remote rural roads in the region, which the local farmers had built and kept up themselves using a mixture of shale, sand, and chert dredged from the Duck River, Sowell Mill Pike was state-maintained. It was wider than Rock Spring Road, so vehicles could go faster, and there was plenty of room for two cars to pass in opposite directions without having to slow down. If you came upon a tractor that was going slowly, you could easily pass it. There was never much traffic on the Pike.

Whoever had built the Pike years before—maybe someone named Mr. Sowell—believed in getting where he was going. The first couple of miles were straight as an arrow, and driving it was fun. The old truck picked up speed as we went down one long hill, then lost its "giddy-up" as we climbed straight up the next hill, until it was barely moving by the time we got to the top. Then we started down again.

As we trundled downhill, I yelled, "Go faster, Grandpa!" But Grandpa pressed the brake, as if reining in a horse that he didn't want breaking into a gallop, and acted like he didn't hear me. He wasn't going to speed up just to entertain his grandson's need for a thrill.

After two miles, we arrived at Union Grove, where the road curved slowly to the left and descended to the Duck River. There, it crossed the Sowell Mill Bridge, which was a strip of concrete so narrow, only one car could cross at a time. It made me wonder if the bridge had originally been built for a horse and wagon. After crossing the bridge, the road ran along a bluff and, after ten miles of dust and heat, dead-ended at the Lewisburg Pike—otherwise known as State Route #234, which led into town from the southeast.

At the spot where the Sowell Mill Pike dead-ended sat an old country store, overgrown with climbing vines, underneath a busted Texaco sign. The building was so old, I thought it might collapse in a strong wind. It seemed to specialize in items for farmers that the grocery stores in town didn't think to stock. I was in a hurry to get to town, but Grandpa stopped at the store, and we went inside to buy a can of blackstrap molasses.

Grandpa paid for the molasses, and we left the store. We got back in the truck, started it up, turned it around, and sat at the intersection where Sowell Mill Pike gave way to the smooth asphalt of the Lewisburg Pike, waiting for an opening that would allow us to merge into the fast-moving traffic on the highway. Whenever we came to that intersection, I had the oddest feeling of leaving behind a time long past—an era of ancient hay balers and horse-drawn wagons, miles of barbed-wire fences, cornbread, and molasses—and stepping into a modern age of gasoline engines and electric lights.

"Be careful, Grandpa," I said. This part of the trip always scared me. The intersection was a dangerous spot. The old truck didn't have much starting-up speed, especially with nothing but loose crushed rock under its worn tires. It sat there idling roughly, hesitant to make a start. Grandma would say that it was trying to "get its gumption up."

Grandpa turned his head, looking both ways twice. Then, with a grinding noise, he put the old truck into first gear and slowly let out the clutch. The truck lurched forward, swaying up onto the shoulder, staggering like an old plow horse that had accidentally stepped into the starting gate at the Kentucky Derby just as the bell sounded. The tired old engine was no longer sure of itself.

The minute we were up on the asphalt surface, a shiny new car charged up on our bumper, looking as if it was about to ram us from behind. At the last moment, it swerved, and the driver laid on the horn as he blew past us on the left. The folks in the car looked annoyed as they passed, as if we were old country hicks who didn't know what we were doing or where we were going. I looked to see what Grandpa thought, but he didn't seem to pay any attention to them. He didn't even glance at them; just kept his eyes on the road ahead.

The transmission made another grinding protest as Grandpa shifted into second gear, then third, and finally fourth, until we were going a respectable forty-five miles per hour, which was about all the old truck could do on its best day. When we'd gone nearly a mile from the old country store, we passed a round sign advertising Nehi Soda that sat up high on a tall pole to our right, welcoming us to the city limits. Finally, after traveling down a long curve to the left, we came to the red light at the corner of East Ninth Street.

When we stopped, Grandpa turned to me and said, "Billy, remember this! Old things that have survived, like this here truck, deserve yer respect, 'cause they've got important lessons t' teach you."

"Lessons like what, Grandpa?"

"Well, fer one thing, they teach you how fast you really need t' go in order t' get t' yer final destination."

He'd lost me. "I don't get it, Grandpa."

"You don't, huh?"

"No, Grandpa. What's that supposed to mean?"

"It means if'n you live yer life at ninety miles an hour, you may get t' yer final destination sooner, but when you get there, you're not gonna know where you've been. You're gonna have been in such a hurry t' get where you were goin' that you'll have arrived and not know why you came. And if'n you go too fast, you just might burn up yer oil, and yer engine's gonna freeze up, so's you never arrive at all."

I didn't understand anything he'd just said. "But Grandpa, what does that have to do with old things? Besides, I kind of like new things. New things can teach you a lot."

"You like new things, huh? That might explain why you never have any money in yer pocket."

"Yeah, maybe." I felt a little bad about always wanting to spend my money, but it was true. Grandma's dollar bill was already talking to my hip bone about its next owner.

He went on. "Billy, it's true sometimes new things can teach you lessons, but new things haven't stood the test of time. So what they have t' teach you hasn't been proved yet. New things are shiny and colorful, and they draw yer attention away from old things that look faded and worn. That's why manufacturers make their products shiny, and box 'um up in bright boxes and wrap 'um as if they were Christmas presents. They do that so's you'll forget about the old things you own that are still perfectly good, and buy their new ones."

I figured Grandpa must know what he was talking about, because he kept all kinds of old things. Dozens of old rusted tools and farm implements hung from the rafters in the old barn, and every now and then, I would come across parts from one of those old devices out in the field, put to some real good use that was completely different from whatever purpose it was first supposed to serve. Grandpa was a genius at seeing new uses for old things. Last year, I'd found a two-foot piece of rubber cooling-hose split lengthwise and fitted around a stretch of barbed-wire fence, right where the wire was fastened to a wooden gate. Grandpa had stripped the hose from the engine of an old tractor that had seen its last days. Now, when he grabbed for the gate to let the cows through, he grabbed the rubber hose, and didn't have to worry about snagging his hand on a razor-sharp length of barbed wire.

"You see, Billy," Grandpa said, "old things have been proven, so they can teach you much more'n new things. Folks who want t' sell you somethin' new tell you on the fancy package how good their new thing is gonna be, but you can't always trust what you read on the package."

I still liked the idea of getting something new, but I was game. "Okay, Grandpa. Show me something old that's stood the test of time."

We were still stopped at the red light on the edge of town, and Grandpa ducked and glanced up through the windshield. "Well, lookie there!" he said. "D'you see those birds sittin' up on that telephone line? They'd be starlings." He pointed up through the windshield.

"Yeah," I said, looking where he was pointing. There must have been thirty starlings sitting on the line.

"Wonder how come all those birds sittin' up on that there line are all facin' the same direction?"

I looked again. Sure enough, they were all facing toward the west.

"How come they're all facing west, Grandpa?"

He just glanced at me. "It'd be a curious thing, don't you think?"

"Yeah, I guess. But I thought we were talking about old things that are real good because they're old, and have something to say to you. Those starlings aren't that old, Grandpa."

"Oh, starlings be real old. Starling-like birds just like those on that telephone line have been 'round fer a million years or more. And you'd just zip right by 'um in yer hurry t' get t' the newest comic books on the rack at Woolworth's five-and-ten-cent store and never stop t' wonder 'bout why those birds be facin' west."

"A million years?" I said.

"Yep. They've been storin' up old wisdom fer generations."

"What kind of wisdom?"

"Wisdom that helps 'um endure," he said.

"Endure? What's 'endure' mean?"

He didn't give me a straight answer. He just said, "Billy, the reason those birds are facin' toward the west is 'cause the prevailin' breeze is blowin' from the west. If'n a hawk is on the hunt and gets t' circlin' high up in the sky on the thermals, and sees 'um restin' on that telephone line, they can take off faster if'n they're facin' into the wind than if'n the wind was at their backs. So they fly off real fast and scatter, and they escape the hawk, all 'cause they've learned through thousands of years t' rest facin' into the wind. It'd be a good lesson fer you."

It was like a lightbulb went off in my head. "I get it, Grandpa! Escaping the hawk means that they've endured."

"Yep! You got it. Those starlings are pretty smart, huh?" Grandpa said. "So you see, you always need t' be facin' in the direction where yer help is comin' from. You need t' keep yer eyes on the things that are gonna make you strong and healthy, things that make life better fer you."

As we moved on from the intersection, I marveled that Grandpa could find a lesson for me in such a small thing as a line of starlings. Nothing meaningful ever seemed to escape his attention. He was like some pioneer hunter constantly on the trail of his next meal, taking clues from every broken twig and every animal track.

We drove across town on Ninth Street. When we finally arrived at the co-op, Grandpa backed the old truck up to the loading platform. We got out, dusted ourselves off, and Grandpa went to introducing his six-year-old grandson to some of the local farmers.

"Afternoon, Joe. This here's my grandson, Billy." Then he turned to me and said, "Billy, this here's Mr. Miller. Mr. Miller's the butcher over at the Piggly Wiggly."

I wasn't sure what to say, so I did my best country imitation and said, "Pleased t' meet you, Mr. Miller," and shook his hand the way I thought I would if I were big. Mr. Miller looked at me, then at Grandpa, and said, "That's a mighty fine young man you got there, Lēgie." He smiled, put his hand on my head, and messed up my hair. I always hated that.

Grandpa didn't linger long. He just tipped his hat to the men, and said to the tallest, "Charlie, hope the missus is feelin' better soon." With that, he left, moving straight to the counter to place his order.

While we were waiting for Grandpa's order to be filled, I tugged on the leg of his overalls. "Grandpa, why didn't you stand and talk with those men for a while?"

"Oh, they just enjoy swappin' stories," he said. "They'll be standin' 'round in a huddle all day, passin' the time t' no good purpose, chewin' tobacco and spittin' into the sawdust on the floor, shootin' the breeze and tryin' t' outdo one another tellin' tall tales. They're like the starlings on the telephone line, 'ceptin' they're all facin' in different directions, goin' nowhere."

"What's wrong with swapping stories?"

"Nothin', long as the stories they be tellin' result in some healthy learnin'. If'n they don't, be best fer 'um t' be makin' new stories with their own hands, doin' the work they've been given t' do."

That was kind of Grandpa's way. No excuse for idle hands. Every job had to have a good purpose. Every story had to teach a lesson. All play had to accomplish some work. For Grandpa, his work was his play. He was intent on creating a new story by making the farm a better place to live, and making the soil more productive. Grandpa's stories were all productive stories.

The cashier at the counter handed Grandpa his bill, which Grandpa paid from a roll of money he pulled from his pocket. After a few minutes, a young man brought the heavy order around to the loading platform on a big hand truck. He stood in amazement as, one by one, Grandpa picked up the ten sixty-pound bags of feed, and then ten bags of fertilizer a hundred pounds apiece, and laid them in the back of the old pickup as if they were grocery bags.

The trip back to the farm that day was pretty ordinary. We stopped by the Piggly Wiggly a block west of the courthouse square on Seventh Street to pick up a crate of Nehi soda. My younger brother Rick and I couldn't do without a Nehi soda to go with our chicken 'n' dumplin's at dinner. We also got some sugar for Grandma, a six-pound bag. It was heavy, but I was proud when I managed to carry it to the truck by myself. And afterward, I talked Grandpa into crossing over West Seventh Street with me, so I could go to Woolworth's and spend the dollar in my pocket. Soon, we were back in the truck and on the way home.

At the edge of town, we passed a big billboard on the right-hand side of the road. The week before, it had displayed a big picture of the Marlboro Man astride his horse, but this week, it was advertising Lucky Strike. Most of the farming men smoked or chewed tobacco. I'd seen them sitting on the courthouse steps, or standing around in huddles in front of church before the Meeting began, and I'd seen them at the co-op.

Grandpa never smoked. As we passed the sign, Grandpa said, "Billy, it'd be best fer you t' turn yer face away from signs like that. Yer help's not comin' from that direction. It'd be best if'n you never go t' smokin' or chewin' tobacco. You just remember the starlings on the telephone line, who've got endurin' wisdom and always be facin' the direction from where their help be comin.'"

He sounded real serious, and I made up my mind right then. If it took the starlings a million years to learn to face into the wind, I figured I could at least spend the summer learning how "facing into the wind" might apply to my young life. I figured I'd probably forget it as soon as I returned to the city. But some lessons stick with you, and to my surprise, I've remembered the lesson of the starlings ever since.

When we got to the turn to get onto the Sowell Mill Pike, Grandpa slowed down some, and the truck dipped and swayed as we left the paved road behind and hit the loose gravel and packed dirt of the roadway. Then he picked up speed, and clouds of dust began swirling up behind us as we made our way back toward Rock Spring. I felt that feeling again—the feeling that we were stepping back in time.

Grandpa sat in silence. Silence was Grandpa's favorite way of speaking, and sitting in the silence was easier to do with Grandpa than with most folks. With Grandpa, you never felt like you had to always be talking just to fill the emptiness.

We rode for a couple of miles, not saying anything. But then he surprised me. Out of the blue, he said, "Billy, there'd be one more important thing 'bout old things that you need t' remember."

"What, Grandpa?"

"What's old be always workin' behind the scenes, even when you're not aware of it. Olde is always at work makin' things better, with or without you."

"I thought everything that was old was past, Grandpa."

"Nope!" he said. There it was again—the dreaded "nope." And he disappeared back into the silence.

We drove on for about another mile, and finally, I took the bait. "Okay, Grandpa. Tell me about something old that's always working."

He thought for a moment, then said, "Well, you remember the earthworms in the garden after Grandma does her hoein'?"

"I hadn't noticed any earthworms when Grandma was hoeing."

"See there!" he said, "You're not noticin' the things right beneath yer own two feet. There are little earthworms in the ground, and most of the time you never notice 'um, but ounce fer ounce and pound fer pound, they can turn over more earth in Grandma's garden in a single day than she can turn over with her hoe workin' all afternoon in the hot sun. Every square yard of Grandma's garden has up t' three hundred earthworms workin' underground, loosenin' and nourishin' the soil. Since Grandma's garden be 'bout sixty square yards, that means that there'd be close t' 18,000 earthworms, all of 'um workin' in Grandma's garden, tillin' the soil from underneath and makin' it better."

Such a big number boggled my mind. "Really, Grandpa?"

"Yep!" he said. "It'd be a fact."

"But Grandpa, earthworms aren't old."

"Sure 'bout that, are you? Of all the things that live on our farm, the earthworms are the oldest. Their kind go back close t' 250 million years. They've endured fer a long time. And 'cause they've got a lotta stored-up wisdom, they have a lot t' teach you."

I couldn't think of anything an earthworm could teach me. But after a silent minute or two, I could tell that Grandpa wasn't going to tell me any more, so I had to prime his pump.

"Okay, Grandpa. Tell me about the lessons an earthworm has to teach me."

"Well, if'n you listen real close t' an earthworm, you might hear him say somethin' like this: 'We've been workin' in this field fer generations, keepin' the soil loose and aerated. You may not notice us, but it's 'cause of us that Grandma can plant and grow watermelons big as a sow's belly, and squash as long as yer arm, and corn as tall as a giraffe's front tooth.' So you see, Billy, you should never assume that a job you're asked t' do is so unimportant that it isn't worth doin' well. Lots of big events depend upon very simple things bein' done first."

Wow, I thought. I had to admit, from the old truck to the starlings on the telephone line, from the farmers shooting the breeze at the co-op to the Marlboro smoking man and the earthworms, it all made a certain kind of sense. I realized that what Grandpa was really trying to tell me was that Olde never got old. Olde just found ways of living into things we called New, so New was always standing on Olde's shoulders. And after I gave it a little more thought, I realized that everything that was new would eventually give way to Olde, and prepare to hoist something new on its shoulders.

And that was my day spent in the old truck, learning all there was to know about Olde from Grandpa—who was old himself. Grandpa was old from the first day I ever knew him, and he was old the whole time I knew him. Maybe Grandpa was Olde—but I didn't think so. When Grandpa spoke about Olde, it sounded like he had someone else in mind.

I had one more question. "Grandpa, how fast does something new become old?"

He kept his eye on the road, but I could see a smile creeping across his weathered face. "In the blink of an eye," he said.

"In the blink of an eye?"

But this time, he didn't reply. He just disappeared back into his silence. His quiet reminded me that there were some questions that I needed to work out on my own. Maybe one day, when I had spent more time with Olde, I would.

Now, It's Your Turn:

_____

_____

_____

_____

_____

_____

_____

_____

_____

_____

_____

_____

_____

_____

_____

_____

_____

_____

_____

_____

_____

_____

_____

3

The Monster Storm of '51

Wisdom from the Farm:

A farm can get outta control in a heartbeat, from flood, fire, drought, and frost; and sometimes it feels like there's nothin' you can do. But remember, you're a force of nature. If'n you're in control of yerself, and become the calm center, others seekin' shelter will be drawn t' you. Blow as hard as it will, no storm can disrupt those people who'd be sheltered in the center of yer calm.

In 1951, on the second Tuesday in July, Mom and Dad dropped me and my brother off at the farm for the summer while they made a trip out west to British Columbia and San Francisco and other places I had never heard of.

A year had gone by in a hurry. I was seven years old, and the number on the inside of my t-shirts had gone up two sizes. I hadn't even noticed that I was getting bigger, but Grandma noticed every year, and told me so: "Billy, you're gettin' t' be bigger than the bunion on Grandpa's big toe."

The summer before, Grandpa had told us that we were living in a log cabin that had been built when Indians still roamed the woods, hunting deer and wild boar. Grandpa said that the house had stood for one hundred and twenty-five years, and just kept getting better and better, 'cause Olde lived in it. Everything about it was old and time-tested.

I wanted to know all about the log cabin, and I had waited a whole year to see the logs.

After breakfast on Wednesday I cornered Grandpa on the front porch. "Grandpa, tell me about the log cabin."

"What log cabin?" he said.

"Come on, Grandpa. Last summer you said you'd show me the log cabin. I've been waiting one-seventh of my whole lifetime to hear about how our farmhouse is really a log cabin." We had studied fractions in school that year, and I wanted to show Grandma, who was a schoolteacher in a one-room school house over in Lickskillet, how much smarter I was getting. "You promised me a whole year ago."

Grandpa smiled at me with a toothpick between his teeth, and leaned his chair back against the wall.

"Okay," he said. "I'll be tellin' it t' you. I guess now'd be as good a time as any."

"This here farmhouse was built 'round 1859, just before the Civil War—or maybe just after the War; we aren't exactly sure 'bout that. It was built by a Mr. Hayes, we think, but we aren't sure 'bout that either; and it was made of logs. We *are* sure 'bout that. In those days, most log cabins were made of logs," he said. He was trying to trick me, and he stopped and smiled to see if I was paying attention.

I was paying attention and said, "Yeah, Grandpa, but where are the logs?

"Oh, the logs are still there. You just can't see 'um. Whoever owned the place after Mr. Hayes covered the logs with yellow poplar planks t' help keep the outdoors out and the indoors in."

"You mean we really are living in a log cabin?"

"Yep," he said.

Grandpa said that with the yellow poplar siding on the outside of the logs, and later, the drywall on the inside, the house was pretty well insulated. Even in the summer, it got cool in the evenings, and Grandpa would build a fire in the fireplace. The heat from the fireplace and the big iron stove in the kitchen kept the whole house toasty warm, except for some drafts that Grandma said were lurking around inside the house and gave people bad colds. Grandma was forever trying to keep my brother and me out of the drafts. "Billy," she'd say, "we gotta stay outta drafts, 'cause a draft be a first cousin t' a cold."

The old house had a hand-hewn, red cedar shingled roof. My dad once told me that a roof shingled in red cedar is good for a hundred years. It doesn't leak. But my dad wasn't there on the night of the monster storm, so he didn't know about the night the cedar shingles met their match.

No doubt about it: the farmhouse was old. It even smelled old, a dank sort of smell. And it was in this old dank and dusty house, on the night of the Monster Storm of '51, that Olde taught me a lesson I will never forget.

That summer, all of us, grandparents and grandkids, slept in the house's east-facing room with its big stone fireplace. There were two beds in that room, and every night, it'd be the same: Grandma would look at Rick and me and say in a whisper, "Which one of you young'uns gonna sleep with yer grandpa tonight?"

Sleeping with Grandpa was dangerous. He was so big and long that he took up most of the bed. His twelve-and-a-half-size feet hung over the end, and when he stretched out full-length, he always pulled the cover off me. If he turned over, his 230 pounds shoved my fifty pounds to the very edge of the bed. Under his considerable weight, the bed sagged some in the middle. Either I'd roll toward him in the night or I had to grab hold of the edge of the mattress and try sleeping uphill. But it was his beard and hairy arms that really got to me. His beard was like a wire brush, even after he'd shaved. He could wear out the edge of a straight razor twice during a single shave.

Neither of us was going to volunteer to contend with that. So Grandma bribed us. She gave a roll of new pennies to the one who would sleep in the bed with Grandpa. My brother and I agreed that it wasn't worth it, so, we met her roll of new pennies and raised her a roll of nickels. We were small, but we weren't dumb.

Some nights, neither of us would take the bribe, and Grandma would send Grandpa to sleep in the attic. He would get the ladder, climb up through the square push-back panel above us on the bedroom ceiling, and with his lantern light, disappear into the darkness.

The attic was very shallow, because the roof had a low profile. It must have been cramped up there, so when Grandpa was sent to the attic, I always felt sad and a little guilty. But secretly, I have to admit I was relieved to see him go.

Out of concern for Grandpa, we asked Grandma what else lived in the attic.

"Ah, nothin' much," she said. "There'd be some hay over the floorboards, and in the hay there might be some mice, and a spider or two. Oh," she added, "and occasionally a snake."

She was just joshing us, I think. Still, it gave me nightmares to imagine Grandpa sleeping up there. In addition to the vermin, it had to be real stuffy. But he never complained, and we never heard him come down once—except on the night of the monster storm.

Each night, while Grandma read us a bedtime story by the light of the Aladdin oil lamp, we would curl up under the sheets and watch the fire in the big fireplace. The fire spat and crackled, and whenever it popped, a small glowing ember went shooting up the chimney.

This particular night, it rained. At first, it was a gentle rain. We could hear thunder off in the distance, but we didn't pay any attention to it. The gentle rain only lasted for ten minutes before it built itself up into a pelting downpour—which was only a prelude to what soon would come.

From out of nowhere, the full force of the storm struck. The pelting downpour became a torrent, sending cascades of water flowing off the edges of the roof and down the windows. Oversized raindrops drummed with a steady, heavy pounding on the roof overhead. By the time the wind arrived, whistling around the corners of the house and screaming like a banshee, I was scared to death. The fire in the fireplace was fighting for its life, making spewing sounds as the rain tried to invade the house through the chimney.

Soon, the torrent became a rampage of pounding water and lightning. Just seconds after each lighting flash, thunder boomed, shaking the whole house. It just kept getting worse and worse—and it went on and on. The old log cabin hadn't seen such conflict since the Civil War.

Under that kind of assault, the hundred-year-old roof was overmatched. Water began to leak through the roofing shakes.

I'd never seen it rain that hard on the farm. The plaster ceiling over the bedroom began to swell up in small, damp circles. The circles grew wider and wider, gathering up water, until a droplet began to form in the middle. In time, the drips fell, splattering on the old, cracked linoleum floor.

We lay in our beds, looking up at the ceiling where, every minute or so, a new damp circle began to form. The lightning struck so close and so bright, it was as if someone was standing outside with a huge camera, popping off flash photos through the window and making the room explode in white.

I felt like we were in the middle of a war. We were under a full artillery assault, and the enemy just kept getting closer and closer. I was soaking wet, and shivering cold. Near tears and afraid, I said, "Grandma, what are we going to do?"

Grandma knew we were afraid. "C'mon now, both of you. I'll show you what we're gonna do!" she said, raising her voice to be heard over the roar of the storm.

"Grandma," I told her as I stood there, shaking, "it won't do any good telling us not to be afraid. That's what grown-ups think—but it doesn't really work."

She surprised me. "Billy," she said, "you go right ahead and be 'fraid all you want. Grandpa and I have done this before." Somehow, her permission to be scared actually helped some with the fear.

Soon the panel overhead opened, and Grandpa climbed down the ladder. His long johns were soaked. He said, "C'mon, 'Ma, we'd best be gatherin' the pots and pans."

"Here's what we're gonna do," she said calmly. "Grandpa's gonna bring the pots and pans from the kitchen, and we're gonna start movin' the beds t' drier areas of the room."

Grandpa soon arrived with his arms full of cooking utensils, they set each one on the floor directly under each of the dripping spots, and the storm just kept coming.

We helped Grandma move the beds to areas of the room that were not yet under the leaks, and as close to the fireplace as possible for added warmth. The storm just got worse. The wind grew stronger, until it became a gale, and great gusts whistled around the southwest corner of the house. The foundation began to creak. A bolt of lightning struck close by and made me jump. We heard a tree topple somewhere outside and crash to the ground with the sound of breaking branches and an earthshaking thud.

Grandma got out of bed again, this time with a little more resolve, and said, "Okay, Grandpa. Get out all my mason jars, bowls, and glass pitchers."

Grandpa left, and came back into the room with an armful of glass jars. The beds were getting wet, so we tried to move them again. By now, there were so many kitchen containers and pots of various shapes and sizes scattered around on the floor that the dripping rain began to sound like a tin-pan symphony, with each instrument tuned to its own pitch.

After what seemed like a couple of hours, it became plain to everyone that trying to contain the water was a losing battle. The rain had breached the old roof, and it was raining on us indoors. The bedsheets were soaked, and so were we. And the storm kept coming. I was terrified to tears, afraid that the storm was going to wash the whole house down the hill, and us with it.

But for Grandma, it was getting to be funny. The helplessness of our situation set her off, and she started into one of her laughing fits.

At first, I looked at her with a question on my face. I didn't see anything funny about our dilemma. But after Grandma got the ball rolling, listening to her laugh was so contagious that I began laughing in spite of myself, right through my tears.

Grandma had the greatest laugh. When she first got tickled her laugh wasn't much more than a giggle, but soon it boiled up into a full-blown laugh until it took over her whole body. She couldn't help herself. If Grandma was standing straight up on her feet when the laughing spell hit her, it would soon cause her to bend over at the waist with her handkerchief over her mouth. Then she'd begin to get short of breath, and she'd gasp for air— but it was no use. Another wave of whatever was funny would hit her in mid-breath, and then she would sneeze. As the fit progressed, her eyeglasses would begin to fog up, and just about the time they did, the hiccups would strike her. Grandma was the only person I ever met who could laugh, sneeze, and hiccup at the same time. Being bent over near double, she'd grab for her glasses with her left hand and for the hem of her apron with her right, trying to sponge away the tears and wipe her nose, which was beginning to leak.

After her laughing fit passed, Grandma was in a playful mood. She got out a bar of soap and pretended to take a shower.

Grandpa overturned a bucket, fixed a five-foot vertical wooden slat to its side, and acted as if he was playing a single-string bass fiddle. You could see him pretending to adjust the pitch of the fiddle by pulling back and forth on the slat, making the string take on more tension or less. He couldn't actually play the thing—in fact, I'd never seen my grandpa make any kind of music, except on one of the hickory whistles he carved for my brother and me—but somehow, the fact that he couldn't play it made it even funnier.

Then Grandma tried to sing "She'll Be Comin' 'Round the Mountain When She Comes," but Grandma had a real bad voice, and we all laughed. Even Grandpa laughed some, which was rare. We had all taken shelter under Grandma's laughing spell.

The rain continued to fall outside, but somehow the roof quit leaking inside. We got some fresh sheets on the beds and finally fell asleep exhausted.

Dawn came, and the rooster climbed up on his fence post and announced the all-clear.

We had a bite of breakfast and then began cleaning up. Grandpa moved all the smaller furniture into the front yard where he wiped it clean with old rags and left it for the sun to dry. Then he took a pail and a mop inside to clean up the water that lay on the floor from the storm. Grandma gathered up all the bedclothes, towels, and blankets, and put them on the back porch where she began washing them and hanging them on the clothesline.

I was helping Grandpa with the furniture cleanup when he said, "Billy, you remember last night how hard you laughed when Grandma had her fit. She was gatherin' you up into her calm. Did she help you forget your fear?"

"Yeah, Grandpa, she did."

"Well, there'd be a lotta things happen on a farm that leave you feelin' outta control: a late freeze, a long drought, the market price of wheat, blight in the trees, cinch bugs in the garden, or a visit from the green tobacco worm. You're always just one crisis away from ruin."

"So, what are you supposed to do when things get out of control?" I asked.

"Not much you can do. Gotta let the flood flood, and the drought drought, and the infested crop infest, and wait fer whatever's outta control t' run its course. Grandma showed you some things last night that you can do, like laugh at yer helplessness, take control of yerself and become a 'force of nature,' and set yer mind t' wait patiently fer the old farm t' compensate you fer yer loss. Last night Grandma didn't just laugh in the face of the storm. She became a 'force of nature.' Billy, did you know that you're a 'force of nature,' too?"

"I am?" I said. "How?"

"Well," he explained, "as long as you're in control of yerself, you'll be creatin' a calm space 'round you. When you create that calm space, other things that are seekin' shelter'll be drawn t' you. So, bein' a 'force of nature,' you have an effect on things 'round you that've gotten outta control.

"And if'n you're a 'force of nature,' it opens the door fer nature t' compensate you. One day nature may give you a goose egg, but the next day, it gives you a plump watermelon. Don't let the goose egg defeat yer spirit. Better t' start watchin' fer yer compensation. And when the watermelon comes, be grateful fer it."

We finished getting all the moveable furniture outside. Then I stretched and yawned, and said, "After being cold and wet, the sun really feels good on my back. Is that a compensation, Grandpa?"

He straightened up and stretched too, his hands high above his head, then lowered them and was immediately overtaken by a deep yawn. My yawn had drawn him in. He smiled and said, "Yep. That'd be a compensation, all right."

Now, It's Your Turn:

_____

_____

_____

_____

_____

_____

_____

_____

_____

_____

_____

_____

_____

_____

_____

_____

_____

_____

_____

_____

_____

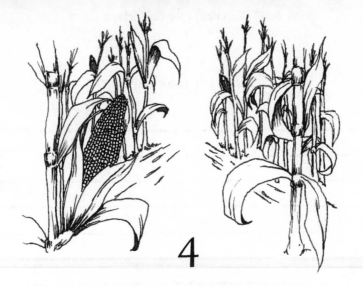

4

Celebrating Christmas with an En-lightened Puritan

Wisdom from the Farm:

Easier may sometimes be faster, but easier's not always better. T' be a caretaker of the soil and the critters that live on it, you have t' practice conservation, and bein' a conservationist means that you have t' go beyond what easy would ask you t' do. Sometimes harder's better'n easier. Doin' things the right way might mean that you have t' choose the harder way, but in the end, it'd be worth it.

It was December of 1952, about a month after my eighth birthday. Around that time in my life, the family typically spent a month with Grandpa and Grandma on the farm. We were seldom there in time for Christmas, but this year, we had arrived early. I wasn't looking forward to Christmas on the farm. In fact, if you didn't know better, you'd never have known it was Christmastime.

On the farm, Christmas was just like every other day. There were no Christmas cards. There was no Christmas tree, and no

Christmas feast. Sometimes, Grandpa brought home a bag of oranges and a box of nuts, just because it was a special day, but he never decorated the house or wrapped a Christmas present.

Once, I'd asked him, "Grandpa, why don't you give presents at Christmastime?"

"You've already got yer Christmas present," he'd said.

"I have?"

"Yep," he said. "You've got yer life, yer strength, yer appetite, and work t' do. So, you'd best be gettin' on with it." Grandpa worked on Christmas Day, and thought everyone else should too.

That year, on Christmas Eve, I asked my dad, "Dad, why doesn't Grandpa like Christmas?"

"Oh, your grandpa likes Christmas, but you might say that he's sort of an 'en-lightened Puritan' when it comes to Christmas."

"What's that mean?"

"Well," Dad said, "The New England Puritans never celebrated Christmas. For them, making a festival out of what was supposed to be the humblest day of the year would've been 'puttin'-on.' They would have looked down their long noses at decorations and said something like, 'Thou shalt not make unto thee any graven image.' Taking the day off, decorating the house, and giving gifts from Santa would've been sacrilegious to the Puritans."

"Oh," I said. "So, why don't we have a Christmas tree?"

"I just told you why."

"You did?" I said. "I don't get it."

"Bill, you don't have to have a tree and presents and such to have Christmas. Your grandfather celebrates Christmas the way they celebrated it in New England." He went on. "Don't misunderstand—Grandpa does observe Christmas. Every year, he buys a dozen Roman candles, and every Christmas Eve, he shoots them off, along with all the other farmers on surrounding farms. After dinner, we'll go out and watch. You'll see."

About an hour later, after it got dark, we all went into the field to watch the spectacle of colored lights as they burst in the sky. One by one, Grandpa lit the end of each big tube and pointed it toward the sky. Each one recoiled with a whoosh, and bright balls of colored fire leapt high into the dark night. Soon enough, they were answered by others, all around the farming community.

It was cold, and as we stood in the field among the stubble left from the harvest of the corn, I looked up at Grandpa and said, "Grandpa, why do the farmers shoot off Roman candles on Christmas Eve, but not celebrate Christmas Day?"

He had a pretty good answer. "The Book says that the night the Lord was born, there got t' be a new light in the sky, and it also says that a new light was comin' into the world. We're settin' off these here candles as a reminder of that holy night. But," he continued, "when the sun comes up tomorrow, a man's meant t' do the work that the Lord has given him t' do."

Grandpa worked from sunup until sundown every day except Sunday; and even on Sundays, there were chores that had to be done. All the livestock had to be tended to every day. Working a farm was different from working a job in the city. If you stopped, even for a day, the farm would get away from you in a hurry and run to thistles, pokeweed, and cactus pods.

Christmas morning passed without incident. Grandpa milked the cows, fed the farm animals, and then drove the cows out to pasture, same as always.

It was true that Grandpa worked all the time, even on Christmas Day. And it was true that he didn't get together with friends to celebrate or throw parties. But he wasn't a Scrooge about it. In school, I had learned that the New England Puritans were all strict and sour-faced, and would often blame others for not being as morally upright as themselves. That didn't sound like Grandpa at all. So, late on Christmas Day before dinner, I asked my dad again what Puritan men were like.

"Dad, tell me again. What's an 'en-light-end Puritan'?"

"Well, it's a Puritan who has seen the light," he said.

Both my grandpa and my dad made a game out of never giving me a straight answer. "C'mon, Dad!"

He went on. "An enlightened Puritan is someone who still values what the old New England Puritans valued, but who has come to see the advantages of breaking with the strictest Puritan beliefs, and is willing to adopt any progressive ideas that have merit. So your grandfather isn't a Puritan like the ones from the old days. In fact, if you ask him if he's a Puritan, he probably won't know what you're talking about."

I thought so. Grandpa wasn't a New England Puritan. He wasn't a real Puritan at all. He just had some ideas that were Puritan ideas. But he liked new ideas, too; ideas that made the soil better for planting and made life around the farm easier for Grandma.

One of those good ideas was electricity. The electric grid hadn't come to that backwoods part of Maury County until 1938, but Grandpa hooked the house to the grid as soon as electricity became available. He put a socket right in the middle of the bedroom ceiling, and had a couple of electrical outlets put into the walls. He screwed a lightbulb into the overhead socket, and plugged electric lamps into the wall outlets. Suddenly, there was light after the sun went down.

Life was easier with electricity. I couldn't imagine what life had been like for Dad, growing up on the farm without it. Bath time would come an hour earlier, and the family wouldn't have time to sit on the front porch listening to the night sounds. Story time would have come earlier and been shorter. Electricity added an extra hour of light in the evening between supper and bedtime, allowing some time at the end of a long day of chores to gather up the events of the day and make sense of it all.

But electricity was expensive, and the Puritans were known for being thrifty. What happened next taught me a lot about Grandpa's Puritan notions.

That school year, I was in the middle of second grade, and I was just learning to read. But reading to yourself was kind of lonely. Stories were always better when I could talk Grandma into reading them out loud to us instead.

It was almost bedtime, and I said, "Grandma, read us a story out of the Indian book." Grandma had a book about the pioneer days in Middle Tennessee, and I loved its stories about settlers and Indians.

Grandma opened the book and settled down to start reading the story, and I leaned eagerly forward. I didn't want to miss anything. But the glare from the bare lightbulb was so bright, I soon found I couldn't think about the storytelling for thinking about how bright the light was.

"Grandpa, can we put a shade over that light?" I said, pointing up toward the ceiling with a finger and shielding my eyes from the glare with my other hand. "It's too bright. It hurts my eyes."

"Does, does it?" he asked.

"Well, can we?"

"Nope!" he said.

"Why not, Grandpa?"

"'Cause 'lectricity costs money, and the bulb does too. So we need t' get all the light we're payin' fer. If'n you go t' puttin' a shade over it, then you're not gettin' all the light that you paid fer, are you?"

"Is that why there aren't any shades on the table lamps?"

"Yup! It'd be all the same."

So at night, before bedtime and 'lights-out,' we lived in the stark light of a bare overhead bulb and two lamps without lampshades on them. That kind of frugality was typical of this en-lightened Tennessee Puritan.

The Sunday after Christmas, we all went to church, parking the car on the grass since there was no parking lot. As we got out of the car, my dad said, "Bill, watch your grandpa at worship this morning. When a Puritan man worships, he doesn't draw any attention to himself. It's a matter of practicing humility."

When it came time for worship, Grandpa sat with the other deacons and elders, up front on the right side opposite the choir. The rest of us sat in the regular pews.

That morning, Grandpa didn't move a muscle during worship. He never raised his hands in praise; he never said 'Amen' like some of the men did, trying to add gun powder to the preacher's fire. He opened the hymnbook, but he didn't sing. Yet in spite of appearances, he was a believing man. I could tell by the way he answered the question I asked him after the service.

When we got home from the Meeting that Sunday, we had dinner—what I usually called lunch. Afterward, everyone took a rest, except Grandpa. He always snuck off somewhere on Sunday afternoons, probably to tend to the farm animals. I never knew for sure. But later that afternoon, I caught him as he was walking up the hill toward the house.

"Where have you been, Grandpa?" I asked him.

"Oh, I've been about," he said. I could tell he wasn't going to answer my question, so I asked another.

"Grandpa, do you believe in God?"

"Yep, s'pose I do," he said.

"That's why you go to church every Sunday, right, Grandpa?"

"Yep," he said.

"Grandpa, tell me about God."

He smiled an off-center smile, and I felt suddenly as if I had stepped onto private property and missed the "No Trespassing" sign.

"A man's standin' with the Lord be a private matter," he said seriously. "Billy, a man's life with God can't be measured by how often he goes t' church, or any holy words that might come outta his mouth. A man's love of God shows in the respect he has fer the Earth and all its critters. A godly man has t' be a steward of the land and live a clean life." He added, "There's a commandment God gave t' Man in the Old Book. It says that we're s'posed t' tend the land fer the Lord 'til He comes again."

Now, that was a lot of words for Grandpa to say all at once. He must have thought that they were real important words for me to hear, or he wouldn't have expended all that energy. Words were precious to Grandpa, and not meant to be wasted. He said listening was dying out from too many folks "speakin' their minds" all at once. Wasting words was wasting good time and energy, and the time would come when a person who wasted words would have to go back and repair any harm that had been done and start over again. Now, that sounded a lot like a Puritan. Maybe Grandpa was an en-lightened Puritan after all.

"Grandpa," I asked, "how come you don't talk much?"

"No need t' talk less'n you have somethin' worth sayin.'"

"I talk all the time," I said.

"I noticed that," he said.

He paused for a moment, looked at me with a smile on his face, and then went on. "Billy, sayin' uncooked words be like ridin' a horse without a bit in its mouth."

I had seen the harnesses Grandpa used with the horses, but I didn't know what the bit was supposed to do. So I asked. "Grandpa, how come you put a bit in the horse's mouth?"

"If'n you put a bit in a horse's mouth, then when you pull gently on the left-hand rein, it pulls the horse's head t' the left; and the horse, bein' a real smart animal, knows that you want him t' turn left. And if'n you pull the rein on the right side, he knows t' turn right. So if'n you put a bit in a horse's mouth, he knows exactly what you want him t' do."

"But what's that got to do with the words I say?"

"Well, if'n we harness ourselves t' the Lord, He can control our tongues, and the Lord can turn us this way and that; but if'n our tongues are unbridled, then our whole body's outta control."

"What happens when we get out of control?"

"Then the words we say get us in trouble, 'cause we don't know what the Lord wants us t' say, so we say the wrong thing at the wrong time, and people can get hurt by the words we say. It'd be better not t' say anythin' than t' say somethin' that might hurt someone."

"But Grandpa, don't you have to talk with people to get to know who they are?"

"Sometimes," he said. "But you can't always tell 'bout a person just by listenin' t' what words are comin' outta their mouths. So talkin' t' a person doesn't always tell you who a person be. You gotta be watchin' what they do. It's what they do that tells you what kinda person they be."

So it turned out this business of not talking too much was a lifestyle for Grandpa. Meanwhile, my wanting to talk all the time caused me to say some uncooked words and ask some stupid questions. Sometimes, I would ask him a question like:

"Grandpa, how come a cow has teats?"

Or: "Grandpa, do you really use cow poop for fertilizer?"

He'd stop and think. You could always tell when Grandpa was thinking. He'd take off his hat and hold it in his hand while he scratched his head, and then he'd decide that it wasn't going to serve any good purpose to answer that question, so he wouldn't say anything. He'd just put his hat back on, and turn and walk away, shaking his head, probably wondering why the Lord had given him such a curious grandson.

That day, we walked on a little further, and I asked, "Grandpa, you just said that the Bible says that we are to 'tend the land 'til the Lord comes.' What does that mean?"

"Means some of the most important work we do in this life is t' take care of the earth."

I could tell from the tone in his voice that "tending the land" was real important to Grandpa. "Yeah," I said, "but how are we supposed to take care of the earth?"

We had reached the steps leading up to the front porch, and we sat down on the top step. Grandpa said, "Takin' care of the earth means takin' care of the dirt, and that means that we do everythin' we can t' keep it fertile, so it'll grow good crops. Fer example, if'n we plant corn on the upper forty every season year after year, eventually the soil gets t' be worn out, and refuses t' grow anythin'. So you tend the land by lettin' it lay fallow fer a season, or plantin' soy fer a year. Soy replaces the nitrogen in the soil and makes it stronger."

"What's 'lay fallow' mean?"

"That just means that you don't plant anythin' on that land fer a season or two. That gives the soil time t' rest."

I didn't understand all the things he was talking about, but I got the gist of it. A Puritan man like Grandpa knew that the dirt got tired if you asked it to grow crops year after year. You had to let the soil rest. I thought that was a pretty good idea.

I figured Grandpa was about talked out, so I thanked him for explaining. And then we got up and went inside and cleaned up for supper.

After supper, I caught up to my dad and told him about my conversation with Grandpa. He nodded along, and told me, "Billy, your grandpa does all kinds of things to make the soil productive. He rotates his crops so that the chemistry of the soil stays rich and fertile. He plants legumes during some seasons to add nitrogen to the dirt. To reduce erosion, he terraces the land,

and he uses certain chemicals like lime to control the pH of the soil. These are some of the progressive steps that an enlightened Puritan man would take to tend the land. Very few farmers in Middle Tennessee are using these new progressive farming techniques. Your grandpa is one of the first."

Dad told me that every year, Grandpa attended the University of Tennessee's Agricultural Extension classes in Columbia and learned about the newest farming methods. In the process, he learned what the soil needed, and how to understand the soil so he could tell what it needed most. Grandpa figured that the soil knew more about what it needed than he did, and that if it tried to speak to him, he'd best listen to it.

That same evening, after my talk with Dad, I found Grandpa on the back porch, sharpening his penknife on a whetstone.

"Grandpa, is the soil a fossil?"

"Yep. The soil be a livin' fossil."

"Living?" That threw me for a loop. "I thought that everything that's a fossil now died long ago."

"Some yes, some no," he said. "A livin' fossil is ancient like other fossils, but it can be brought back t' life, so's it becomes somethin' that lives and breathes and creates new growth. But it needs our help if'n it's gonna be a livin' fossil."

I'd seen Grandpa help the soil before. When we were walking in the fields, he would sometimes bend down and take a clump of it in his hand, and break it apart to test its texture. I'd even seen him smell it, checking to see whether it was able to hold moisture. Grandpa said that when he smelled the soil, it talked to him and told him what hardships it had endured in the past, and what kinds of nutrients it needed in order to come alive again. Grandpa said that feeding nutrients to the dirt so that it could become good soil again was called "tending the soil."

Later that evening, just before the sun set, Dad stopped me after supper, handed me my winter jacket, and suggested we take a walk.

It was unusual for Dad to ask me to walk with him, so I was a little anxious about where this was leading. We set off down the hill toward the barn. It would be dark soon, and Dad hadn't brought a lantern, so I knew the talk was going to be short and serious.

"Bill," he said, "do you remember the sermon from yesterday?"

"Yes," I lied.

"What did the preacher say?"

I should have seen that one coming. I said, "I don't remember, Dad. I was busy watching Grandpa."

"So you told a little lie there, didn't you?"

"I guess. But I didn't hurt anybody."

"No, but you hurt your soul some, didn't you? Grandpa talked to you about tending the soil; well, what we're talking about now is called "tending the soul." That's what the preacher was saying yesterday. You need to always be examining your soul, just like you check the soil. If you don't feed your soul, it will stop producing good things in you. Do you see that?"

With a hangdog expression on my face, I said, "Yes, sir." I didn't know what else to say, so I just hung my head. I didn't think I had really done anything wrong, so I was beginning to feel a little angry at Dad for catching me in such a small deception. But if I got angry at my dad for pointing out how easily a lie could take root in my soul like a weed, then I wouldn't be tending my soul, and that would lead to bad things. So I didn't argue with him.

Turned out he was setting me up for another lesson about Puritan men. "Bill, ever since we arrived on the farm you've been asking me about Grandpa and the Puritans. The New England

Puritans practiced a strict code of something called personal conduct."

"Dad, what's personal conduct?"

"Well, that's conduct that's personal," he said.

Dad could tell I was a little frustrated. So he hurried on and told me what he meant. "The Puritans in New England got to the point where they wanted to press their 'ethic' on all those around them, which means they were willing to rise to high political office in order to impose their own standards of personal conduct upon others by way of governance. Now, Bill, your grandpa has a personal code of behavior, and he lives it to the letter. He doesn't smoke. He doesn't drink. He doesn't curse. He's faithful to one wife. But he never imposes his standards on anyone. Grandpa's too much a man favoring religious freedom to impose his religion on others, and too much a Baptist not to value freedom. He respects others who choose to live by a different standard, even though he wouldn't join them, just to be sociable."

We turned around and climbed the hill back to the farmhouse. The lesson was over. I was exhausted. All this talk about why Grandpa worked on Christmas Day, and about harnessing our words so they don't hurt someone, and tending the soil, and personal conduct, and respecting others had really worn me out.

It was too cold that night for the family to sit on the porch, so we went inside, and Grandpa made a fire in the big fireplace in the bedroom. I listened to my radio shows, crawled under the covers, and called it a day. The next thing I knew, the rooster was on his fence post, announcing the arrival of Tuesday morning.

That day, Grandpa and his brother Calvin were going to a farm auction. They'd be gone till late afternoon. I wanted to go, but Dad said I would be "underfoot." So instead, after breakfast,

Dad asked me if I would like to go to the shed where Grandpa kept the farm machinery and ride the old tractor.

I was excited. I knew that Grandpa owned an old tractor, but he never used it, and I'd never seen it. What I didn't know was that the old tractor had one more lesson to teach me about the en-lightened Puritan.

After Dad tied up his boots, we started off toward the shed south of the farmhouse. We walked through the orchard, along the ridgeline, and then downhill to the shed. On the way, Dad told me about Grandpa's tractor.

"Bill," he said, "Your grandfather was the first farmer in the area to purchase a tractor. It was a Fordson tractor, and was one of the first tractors ever made by the Ford Motor Company."

"Does it still run?" I asked.

"Grandpa keeps it in running condition, but it's over thirty years old. He bought it all the way back in 1921, about four years after they had come on the market. Paid $750 for it, brand-new. He'd been studying the tractor, and thought that it might make work on the farm easier and better. It had a twenty-horsepower, four-cycle vaporizing oil engine that ran from two to six miles per hour, with a worm-gear reduction set in the differential."

"Sounds like a real complicated machine," I said.

"That was the problem," he said.

We arrived at the shed. Dad took the padlock off the doors—and there it was.

The tractor was showing its age. Most of the tractor had rusted, except the seat and the big steering wheel. Dad added some oil and filled the coolant system with water. Then he topped off the fuel tank with kerosene. The tractor squeaked as he climbed up and sat in the seat. He switched on the ignition, pulled the choke out some, and then got down and went around the front to where the crank was.

It took three tries to get the tractor to start. It sounded real loud, and when it had warmed up some, Dad put it in gear and drove it into the grassy field just beyond the shed. Once it was outside, the noise wasn't as loud, and Dad could hear me when I shouted, "Dad, can I drive?"

"Come up here and sit with me. You can steer while I operate the clutch and the gearbox."

I stepped on the drawbar at the back of the tractor and worked my way around to where Dad was until I was sitting on the front edge of the seat. I grabbed the steering wheel and pretended I was in a race, until Dad stopped me. "This tractor isn't a toy, Bill. If you want to steer, you'll have to do it properly."

We drove that tractor all over the small field in front of the shed. Forward, backward, in circles. We pretended we were plowing a field. It was great fun, and Dad told me that when he had been a young man, he had plowed the fields many times with this old tractor. We drove the tractor until its engine began to get too hot, and then shut it off to let it cool.

By that time, it was midafternoon, and Dad said that Mom and Grandma might be needing us for something back at the house. So we backed the old tractor into the shed, and Dad closed the wooden doors, and put the padlock back on the latch.

"How come Grandpa never uses the tractor anymore?" I asked.

"That's a question you'll have to ask him," he said.

"I'll ask him as soon as he gets home from the farm auction," I said.

"You'd best wait until tomorrow. When Grandpa gets home later this afternoon, he's going to have a lot of things to take care of before dark. Let's leave Grandpa to get his work done tonight. You'll have plenty of time tomorrow to talk to him about the tractor."

As we walked back uphill to the farmhouse, Dad said, "Bill, before you ask Grandpa about the tractor, ask him whether he ever had any mechanical horses on the farm."

"Why should I do that?" I asked.

"Well, the tractor is a twenty horse-power machine. It has the equivalent power of twenty horses. Grandpa knows that we started the old tractor up this afternoon. Let's see if he guesses what your question is really about."

When we got back to the house, Grandma took one look at my dirty clothes and the smudges of oil and rust all over my arms and face, and put me in a washtub full of hot water for an early bath. By the time Grandpa got home, there was only an hour of light left before the sun went down, so, Grandpa drove the cows in from the pasture and did the milking. Then he came up to the house for a late dinner. He didn't say a word about the auction. I guessed that being with Uncle Calvin all day must have worn him out.

After dinner, Grandpa built a fire in the big stone fireplace and Grandma got us ready for bed and read us a story. After the story, I just lay there in the bed and watched the fire and the next thing I knew, the rooster was up on his fence post and it was Wednesday morning.

After breakfast, I caught up to Grandpa as he was trying to fix up a hydraulic pump that would help pump water from the spring up the hill to the house. I couldn't wait to ask him my father's question.

"Grandpa, in the old days, did you have any mechanical horses on the farm?"

"Yep," he said.

"What kind of horses?"

"Mechanical horses."

"Mechanical horses?" I wondered if he had already talked to Dad about the tractor.

"How many horses did you own?" I asked.

"'Bout twenty," he said, smiling that slight smile of his, which usually meant he was way ahead of me.

Grandpa told me about his first tractor, and how it had made farming easier. That was when I played my trump card. "Grandpa, if it was easier to plow with the tractor, how come you went back to plowing with mules?"

I was proud of myself. I had set up the whole conversation so Grandpa would tell me why the tractor was sitting unused out in the shed, going to rust.

"The mechanical horses were always breakin' down. And you'd have t' send off t' the big city fer a replacement part, and when it finally came, it'd be the wrong part, so you'd have t' send off again and wait 'n' wait, hopin' it'd come before the frost set in."

"So plowing with the mules really was easier," I said.

"'Twasn't easier, 'twas better," he said.

"Why isn't easier better, Grandpa?"

"'Cause if'n you feed 'um and treat 'um right, a mule doesn't break down. With a good mule, you can be workin' the land whenever you need t' be."

That made sense, and I learned a lesson. "Easier" doesn't always mean "better." Sometimes "easier" means getting things done faster with less energy spent. You might even get up to six miles per hour—but that would be moving faster than farm speed. You'd be getting ahead of the farm, and wind up having to wait for a couple of days for the spirit of the soil to catch up to you.

"Farm speed"—that was the speed that a farmer had to maintain if the farmer was going to keep up with the growth of the crop. Farm speed was slow and deliberate. There was planting that had to be done; and then cultivating; and then, months later, harvesting. But I was always in a hurry, and to me, farm speed was so slow that it made life boring. In the city, one thing happened so close to the next that if you didn't have a schedule, you'd miss an important appointment.

Grandpa didn't keep that kind of schedule. There were always things that needed to be done, but if you got to going too fast and got ahead of the farm, you could do a lot of damage to the crops and the animals. If you got in a hurry and cut the ear off the stalk before the tassel turned, the corn wouldn't be good. If you got in a rush and went into the henhouse too early, the hens wouldn't have time to get their laying done. If you milked the Jersey before she had a day to graze, you wouldn't get milk.

But there was still one point about Grandpa's philosophy that bothered me. "Grandpa, it seems to me that the faster you can get your chores done, the more time you have to play," I said.

"Thought it might seem that way t' you," he said.

"Billy, if'n you do it right, it may take longer, and you'll be more tuckered out when you finish; but you'll have the satisfaction of havin' done it right."

I remembered that Dad had told me that working easier wasn't something that normally appealed to the Puritan man. There was something about "easier" that really meant "cutting a corner," so you wouldn't have to work so hard. "And if'n you have the satisfaction of doin' somethin' right," Grandpa continued, "then yer work will seem like play."

I didn't have an answer for that one. Maybe one day, when I'm all grown up, I thought, the work I do will seem like play. Right then, the work I watched Grandpa do every day looked like work, not play. Maybe being a child was a time when I was supposed to work at playing, and when I got to be a grown-up, I'd play at working.

Maybe I'd never be a farmer. I didn't think I had the patience for it—still don't. But even then, I knew I would like to grow up to be like Grandpa.

Now, It's Your Turn:

_____

_____

_____

_____

_____

_____

_____

_____

_____

_____

_____

_____

_____

_____

_____

_____

_____

_____

_____

_____

_____

_____

_____

_____

_____

5

The Barbershop: My First Close Shave

Wisdom from the Farm:

Fear comes from forgettin' yer deliverances. After you've been delivered from some fearful moment in yer life, you feel a sense of relief and tell yerself that what you first feared wasn't as fearful as you first feared it would be. If'n you can remember the "after feeling" and put it ahead of the "before feeling" then, when you face a new fear, it'll help you manage yer fear, and you won't feel as frightened as you thought you'd be.

By the time I was eight years old, I'd been to the barbershop with Grandpa lots of times—but that year marked the first visit to the barbershop that I can still recall to this day. On that occasion, I went with Grandpa expecting to watch him get a shave and haircut, just as I did every Saturday. But this particular Saturday, Grandpa had something else in mind.

The faded green pickup truck carried us into town with its usual clank and rattle. Once we'd parked, Grandpa came around the back of the truck, took me by the hand, and led me toward the barbershop on the opposite end of the square.

Beside the door to the barbershop stood a big candy-cane pole that turned inside a glass tube. The tube looked like it was spinning up into the sky, but it never moved up. It just looked like it would.

I didn't remember seeing the barber pole during earlier visits to the barbershop, but on this occasion, I noticed it. With my free hand, I pointed to the candy cane tube and said, "Grandpa, how come that barber pole looks like it's going up, but never does?"

"It'd be an optical illusion," he said. Grandpa had an inquisitive mind. These things fascinated him as much as they did me.

"What's an optical illusion, Grandpa?"

"An optical illusion is a trick that yer eyes play on you," he said.

"How's that a trick?"

"It'd be a trick 'cause the stripes on the pole fool yer mind's eye into thinkin' the pole is goin' straight up in the air, but it really isn't," he said. "The barber pole has an interesting history. Years ago barbers used t' dabble in surgery, like pullin' teeth and such, and when a bandage got bloody, they'd wrap it 'round a white pole, like it was spiralin' upward."

"Why'd they do that, Grandpa?"

"They did it t' lift the spirits of the fella who just got a tooth pulled," he said.

I stopped and pulled on Grandpa's hand. I had a loose tooth, right in the lower front. Mom said that a permanent tooth was going to arrive soon and take its place. It wasn't too loose yet, but it would be just like my grandpa to lure me into a place where they'd pull that tooth right out of my head, just to speed up the healing process.

"Grandpa, I don't feel like going into the barbershop today."

He must have guessed what I was thinking, because he kneeled down and said, "Billy, when I was yer age and I had a loose tooth, my dad would tie a string 'round my tooth and tie the other end of the string t' a doorknob on a door that wasn't quite closed. Then he'd sit me in a chair and slam the door, and the tooth would pop right out before I even knew what was happenin'. And the biggest surprise was that it never hurt near as bad as I thought it would."

That did it. I pulled harder. "No, Grandpa, I'm not going in!" And I really meant it. The image of the doorknob and string made up my mind for me.

Grandpa looked me in the eye and said, "Now Billy, remember, the barber pole is s'posed t' lift yer spirits, 'cause a barbershop is a happy place. Remember last Saturday, we went in t' see the barber, and everyone was laughin' and tellin' jokes and kiddin' you 'bout bein' old enough t' get yer first shave?"

"Yeah, Grandpa, I remember."

"Well, you didn't see 'um pullin' any teeth last week, did you?"

"No, but...."

"And you didn't see any bloody bandages layin' 'round, did you?"

"No. But...."

"You just come along with Grandpa, and lift yer head up and walk through that door with yer smile curlin' up from ear t' ear just like the barber pole, and everythin's gonna be alright. You'll see."

I could never say no to Grandpa for long. Even though I still felt a little scared by all that talk about blood and pulling teeth, I said, "Okay." And, gathering up all the courage I could, I went into the barbershop with the biggest smile I could muster plastered across my face.

When we opened the door, bells jangled to announce our coming, and the aromas of talcum powder and lilac water smelled fresh on the air. Every barber chair but one was filled, and in the waiting area, only two of the eight cushioned chairs sat empty. Saturday was always a busy day at the barbershop because everyone was getting ready to go to church the next day.

When we came through the door, the barbers said, "Hey, Lēgie. Good t' see you."

And when they saw me, they didn't say things that grown-ups usually say to children, like "look how much you've grown." They said, "Hey, Billy, has yer Grandpa let you fire the shotgun yet?" Or, "Mornin' Billy, good lookin' fella like yerself, bet you've got girlfriends hangin' on both arms." They made me feel grown-up.

"Lēgie!" they said. "We heard you took Billy down t' the mule auction last Thursday. How'd you like that, Billy? Kinda hard fer a man t' breathe in a place like that, with all the dust and all." But they didn't wait for an answer. They started talking about a redistricting proposal for some property just inside the city limits, and they lost me.

Grandpa took off his hat and hung it on one of the hooks on the wall. Then he took a seat in the chair nearest the window. I was wearing a pull-over t-shirt with broad brown and yellow horizontal stripes, so I didn't have anything like a hat or a coat to hang on the wall hooks. I looked down at my sneakers and wished that I'd worn my Sunday shoes, so that I could walk to the far end of the barbershop and sit in the shoeshine chair. Alvin, the shoeshine man, was a real artist, and could make a pair of old leather shoes shine brighter than the day they first came out of the box. If he had shined my shoes, I'd have worn them to church the next day and been real proud. Instead, I moved an empty chair close to Grandpa and sat down beside him.

Joe, one of the barber men, looked at me as we were sitting there. "Billy, why you got that silly grin on yer face?"

I answered him with a shrug and tried to tone down my smile a bit.

Chairs lined the length of the wall on the left side of the room, and there were a couple of small tables full of old magazines lined up in front of the chairs. Grandpa took up a copy of the *Daily Herald* from the table and commenced reading. I would have joined him, but the smoke from the cigars and cigarettes that the men were smoking was making my eyes sting, and I wondered if the maple-colored wood paneling that stretched the length of the shop had aged a couple of shades darker from all the smoke.

There were three men ahead of us waiting to get their hair cut. One man folded his newspaper, and talking to no one in particular, commented about the high price of feed at the co-op. His comment hung in the air until it encountered the thought of another farmer, and a friendly conversation broke out.

One thing that was constant in the barbershop was the talk. The talk at the barbershop was almost always good-natured banter. Some of it was personal, as one farmer asked another about the welfare of a family member; and some was about farming talk that I didn't understand—talk about wheat not giving an equitable return on the bushel, and corn being up to five dollars on the barrel (which was five bushels), pork futures, and such.

I turned to Grandpa. "Grandpa, what are pork futures?"

He shuffled the pages of the newspaper until he got to the business section and showed me an article: "Pork Futures Up Two Points Since the First of the Week." He said, "Billy, d'you see all these men readin' the newspaper?"

I looked around the barbershop, and sure enough, most of the men in the shop were reading the paper. "Yeah, Grandpa, I see."

He said, "Knowin' what's goin' on in a small farmin' community like ours is important. We're a close-knit community, and what happens t' one of us tends t' affect all of us. Look here," he said, and he pointed to an article in the section labeled "Goings-On Around Town." "This here paper is full of stories 'bout what's happenin' t' folks 'round town, and we know all these folks. Fer example, look at this one." He showed me an article right under a picture of a woman whose name was Mrs. Adele Palmer.

I tried to read what it said. "'Mrs. Adele Palmer is entertaining her daughter Sue and her son-in-law Jack, who are in town to visit on the occasion of Adele's seventieth birthday. Sue and Jack Jackson have just arrived from Memphis and are staying until next Tuesday before they drive home. Mr. Jackson, Adele's son-in-law, has just been promoted to the position of executive manager at the First Union and Trust Bank in Memphis.'"

I had just finished second grade, so I stumbled on some of the big words. But it made me feel good when Grandpa said, "'That'd be really good readin', Billy.'"

He went on, "Now, here's what happens. After we get a shave and a haircut, we're gonna walk over t' the Woolworth store, and chances are we're gonna run into Mrs. Palmer on the sidewalk, and you're gonna speak right up and say, 'Happy birthday, Mrs. Palmer. I see that yer daughter and her husband are in town fer the happy occasion. Sue's done really well marryin' such a smart fella. I heard 'bout his promotion t' executive manager at the bank in Memphis. Congratulations, I reckon yer right proud of him.' That's gonna make Mrs. Palmer feel real good, and she's gonna say, 'Well, aren't you the most thoughtful young man. I'll bet yer grandfather is real proud of you.'"

I would have responded, but Grandpa was already off, deep into a newspaper article about the upcoming University of Tennessee farm extension weekend, and I was getting bored and restless.

As I sat there waiting for one of the barbers to call Grandpa's name, I surveyed the long mirror that ran all the way down the wall on the right side of the room behind the barbers. On a glass shelf underneath the mirror were rows of bottles full of colored water: purple lilac-scented water, green mint-scented water, brown musk-scented water, and several others. The mirror reflected images of the bottles, so that it looked like there were two of each bottle standing side by side; and when the sunlight came through the big front window and struck the bottles, they flashed and made little tinted rainbows in the mirror. It made for a real festive mood, and I loved watching the colors dancing behind the barbers' chairs.

About this time, Jake, one of the barbers, said, "Okay, Ralph, your turn. I been savin' this chair just fer you."

Ralph laid down the newspaper, crossed the room, and took his seat in the empty barber chair while Jake got fresh sheets and towels out of the cupboard. Roy got his hat off one of the hooks and turned to leave the shop, Hank, another of the barbers, hollered after him. "Lookin' forward t' droppin' by yer vegetable stall and checkin' out yer melons!"

Roy said, "We've set up our stall 'bout halfway down Main Street. C'mon by, and I'll show you a canter-melon bigger'n yer belly."

Everyone got a chuckle out of that, even Grandpa. Grandpa had a strange sort of laugh. When he heard something funny, a shallow grin would slowly spread across his weathered face, exposing his teeth—of which he had lost a few. When Grandpa laughed, his eyes always sparkled like he was learning something new that he'd never thought of before. His shoulders would rise and fall once or twice as the laughter shook his body, but not much laughing noise ever came out of his mouth. What did come out was a low, hoarse, gravelly sound that was as rough on the inside as his beard was on the outside. His laugh was short-lived, just one or two heaves of the diaphragm, and he was done. His laughing time was so short, you had to add in the smile as part of the laughter, or you'd miss it altogether.

As soon as Roy left the shop, accompanied by another jangling of the bells, two of the barber-men, Hank and Jake, began poking fun at each other. Barber Hank said, "I watched how you just shaved Roy. If you had a razor in each hand, his beard would still grow so fast you couldn't keep up with it if you had all afternoon. Jake, you'd make Roy late for dinner."

Jake took that as a friendly barb, and he took up his razor, put some shaving cream on it, and flipped it at Hank, hitting him in the ear. Once again, everybody laughed, including Hank.

Then Jake and Hank tried to outdo each other telling jokes. Jake said to Hank, "Hank, did I tell you how poor I'm gettin' t' be? Well, I'm tellin' you, if a fat goose were ten cents a pound, I couldn't buy a hummingbird."

Everybody got a chuckle out of that.

Not to be outdone, Hank said, "Hey Jake, you think you're poor; well, if'n I could go 'round the world for ten dollars, I couldn't get outta sight."

And everybody broke down laughing at that one. But Grandpa didn't laugh. He just smiled that smile of his and went on reading the newspaper.

Sitting there, I realized that Grandpa was right: there was always laughter in the barbershop. It really was a happy place. The jokes that the men told made the day feel more cheerful.

Finally, Joe called out, "Lēgie, you're up."

Grandpa put down his newspaper and took a seat in the barber chair—the kind that ratcheted up, so that after you sat down in it, the barber could pump and pump the handle on the side of the chair until you were high enough off the ground that he wouldn't have to bend over to cut your hair. Behind each chair was a sink, so that the barber could lower you backward and wash your hair under the warm running water.

I watched as Joe adjusted the chair so that Grandpa would fit right into it. In Grandpa's case, being as tall as he was, the barber had to lower the chair. Then he took a big white sheet and put it over Grandpa, pulling it up around his shoulders, and stuffed the edge into Grandpa's collar so as to catch all the loose hair.

There was a wide leather strop attached to the side of Joe's barber chair, and Joe took his straight razor and slapped it up and down the leather strop, making the cutting edge of his straight razor so sharp that it glistened in the light. I tried not to watch, but I couldn't help myself. I was afraid of the razors that the barbers used. I knew that if Joe's hand slipped even a little bit while he was doing the shaving, he might nick Grandpa in the throat.

I watched as Joe lathered up Grandpa's face with a soft brush. Then he lifted Grandpa's chin up so that he could put that blade right up against his throat. I tried to see what Joe was doing but couldn't bring myself to watch, so I looked away. After a couple of minutes, I looked up. Joe had finished the shave, and hadn't nicked Grandpa a single time. I was glad that was over.

Next came the steaming hot towel, which scared me almost as much as the razor. Joe wrapped the towel in a kind of beehive shape, so that it completely covered Grandpa's face, including his mouth and nose. Steam rose off the towel, and I didn't see how Grandpa could breathe. I was real glad that it was Grandpa, not me, who was getting a shave and a haircut.

After a couple of minutes, Joe took the towel off, splashed some of the colored water on his hands, and then slapped

Grandpa lightly on the face. Next, he stepped on a pedal on the back of the barber chair, laid the chair back so that Grandpa's head was over the sink, and washed Grandpa's hair. Then Joe stepped on the pedal again, and the chair sat upright. Joe commenced to cutting Grandpa's hair. Grandpa had so little hair that I thought the barber should have given him a discount on the haircut.

Finally, after carefully taking the sheet off of Grandpa so that he didn't get loose cut hair all over his clothes, Joe shook some talcum powder down the back of Grandpa's collar, and the whole process was over.

After Grandpa stepped down out of the barber chair, the barber lifted the white sheet up into the air and then brought it down hard, with a crack. That got all the loose hair out before the next customer came. It sounded like a rifle shot, only not as loud.

Suddenly, Grandpa turned to me and said, "Okay, Billy, yer turn. Get up in Joe's chair. 'Bout time you had a proper shave, I 'spect."

I looked up at Grandpa with my heart in my throat. Maybe the whole venture really had been designed to trick me into getting my tooth pulled.

Shaking my head, I said, "No, Grandpa. I don't want to."

But he picked me up and set me in the chair anyway. He put his hand behind his ear and said, "Wha'd you say? I didn't get that last part."

Now, the one thing I always wanted was to show my grandpa that I wasn't afraid of anything. Odd—since the truth was, I was afraid of almost everything! I had been scared to death the day I'd stepped on a snake in a patch of grass down by the creek, but I'd gathered up my "gumption" and showed him I wasn't afraid. And I'd pretended to look at the black widow spider that he'd caught and put in a glass jar, when I hadn't even wanted to see the thing. When Grandpa opened the hive, and the bees had swarmed all around him, I stood still like it was something I did every day. No problem.

So when Grandpa picked me up and set me in Joe's chair, I used my imagination and put on that funny smile I'd used walking into the barbershop so he wouldn't think I was scared.

"How long since you had a decent shave, Billy?" Barber Joe said to me. And as he asked me, he flashed the straight razor at me from the inside of his palm.

I was definitely afraid of that razor. Suddenly, I could feel my heart beating faster in my chest, and I couldn't catch my breath. Without much breath, I couldn't holler for help. All I wanted to do was run. But Grandpa was sitting in one of the chairs in the waiting area, watching, so I held it all together like a man—even though I was too petrified to say a thing in response to Barber Joe's question.

Barber Joe threw a fresh sheet around me, pulled it up around my neck, and tied it tight in the back. Then he ratcheted the chair up high, giving me an entirely new perspective on the barbershop. Using a small round brush, he covered my cheeks and neck and under my nose with foam he had stirred up in a shaving mug. The razor made a slapping sound as he stropped it on the leather strop. Then he waved it in front of my face, lifted my chin so I couldn't see, and placed that razor next to my throat. I panicked.

I wanted to scream for help, but with my chin lifted up so high, I couldn't get any noise to come out. I managed a short, muffled protest, which nobody heard over all the barbershop talk. I didn't dare move. If I did, the razor would cut me for sure.

Joe began to shave off the heavy cream. Since I couldn't see, I didn't know it, but Joe wasn't using a razor. When I wasn't looking, he had picked up a black comb, and pressed its teeth against my skin. After he had removed the foam from under my chin, he raised the comb in front of my face where I could see it before he began to "shave" my cheek. When I saw that it was only a comb, I felt instant relief, and all the barber men laughed.

I guess it was kind of funny, but I didn't laugh. My heart was still beating fast, and I still felt the leftovers of that panicky feeling in my chest.

I let Barber Joe shave the rest of my face, scraping away the shaving cream while everybody watched. Grandpa smiled, and his shoulders jumped once or twice as he laughed his silent laugh. He nodded as he looked at me, and his eyes sparkled.

The next obstacle to overcome was the hot towel, which I dreaded almost as much as the blade of the straight razor. The barber wrapped the towel around my face. For an instant it was fiery hot, but it quickly cooled to soothing and warm, and I found I could still breathe. It wasn't as hot as I'd thought it would be.

When Joe took the towel off, the air in the barbershop felt cool on my face. Then he splashed some lilac water on my cheeks. It didn't sting like I had expected, and the smell of it made me feel fresh all over.

Then, without warning me, Joe laid the chair backward. I grabbed the arms of the chair, feeling like I was falling. He lowered my head to the level of the sink and washed my hair in warm water. It felt good. I was beginning to relax.

Finally, Joe lifted the chair until I was sitting up straight and cut my hair with real barber's scissors. He lifted the back of my shirt collar and dusted me with talcum. He pulled off the white sheet and lowered the chair, and I hopped out, a new man.

The great blessing of the event came when we opened the door to leave the barbershop, and a cool, dry summer breeze hit me. I have seldom felt as fresh and clean as I did at that moment. The whole world smelled like a spring day in May, and I felt happy again.

That day, I learned for the first time that I didn't have to live with my fear. I found instead that when I faced it and walked through it, there was a happiness on the other side.

After my barbershop experience, Grandpa took me across the street to the Woolworth's, where he sat me on a bar stool up next to the counter and bought me an ice-cream soda, and some comic books for the trip home. As I sat at the soda fountain and enjoyed my ice cream, I thought about my adventure in the barbershop, how fearful I had been, and how Grandpa had helped me get through it. I knew right then that I would never fear the barbershop again.

And that's the lesson about facing fear. If you just trust whoever is trustworthy around you—and you can always find someone trustworthy, especially if you have faith in God—then on the other side of the fear, there's usually a time of deliverance and refreshment, and the whole world seems new again. If you could just remember the "after" part before the "beginning" part, you wouldn't be so afraid. I've just always had trouble remembering the "after" part when I'm at the beginning. I still get fearful about a lot of things, but I keep working on it.

As we came out of Woolworth's and crossed the street to the green pickup, I looked up at the barber pole still spinning up toward the sky. It made me remember the conversation we'd had before, and I had to ask one more time: "Grandpa, what's an optical illusion?"

"It'd be when you let yer smile curl up, 'cause you know that things are gonna turn out just fine, even when you're thinkin' they're not. You see, Billy, not much ever turns out t' be as bad as you think it's gonna be."

Now, It's Your Turn:

_____

_____

_____

_____

_____

_____

_____

_____

_____

_____

_____

_____

_____

_____

_____

_____

_____

_____

_____

_____

_____

_____

6

What Was Seen and Heard
from the Front Porch

Wisdom from the Farm:

Noticin' be more'n a "glance here" and a "lookie there."
T' really notice, you have t' be still and gaze at somethin'
with all yer receptors focused. Then you can see the Extra-
ordinariness at the heart of everythin' that looks plain
and ordinary. It can be hard work, but if'n you learn t'
notice, the world will come alive fer you in ways you never
imagined.

E very evening as the day cooled down, the family would
gather on the front porch and sit in old rocking chairs
in the midst of Grandma's morning glories, which were already
closing for the night. It was a family tradition. The fading
sunlight backlit the tall fir trees five hundred yards away across
the road that ran by the foot of the hill. Just after dark, the night
sounds would erupt: owls, bats, frogs, the last bawling of the
cows, and the chirping of the chimney swifts settling down in
their nest inside the old stone chimney that stood at the back

of the house. The crickets would sing out, too, with their high-pitched song turned up real loud.

This was the one time that the grown-ups got together and caught up on the events of the day, so my brother and I tried not to interrupt. We just rocked quietly, listening, and waiting for the lightning bugs to turn themselves on. But what we were really waiting for were the radio shows that came on the big Philco radio every night—*Amos and Andy, Jack Benny, The Shadow Knows,* and my personal favorite, *The Lone Ranger.* Each night around 7:00 p.m., the radio ears would begin to gather words out of the air. Every thirty minutes, a new program was broadcast, back to back to back until the radio went off the air at 9:00 p.m. Rick and I never missed a night.

Listening to the radio was much more interesting than listening to the grown-ups talk. Normally, porch conversations dealt with grown-up affairs that I didn't understand and people in the community I didn't know. But one warm night in July when I was nine years old, after we'd been on the farm for a couple of weeks, the adults didn't seem to have much to say, and their long silences allowed the night critters to take the stage. That was the night I broke my silence.

"How come the crickets are so loud on the farm?" I blurted out to no one in particular.

No one had been expecting Rick or me to say anything, so I took them all by surprise. After a moment, Grandma said, "They're always this loud."

"Not where I come from," I said, more abruptly than I should have.

Grandpa said, "You don't practice yer hearin' enough."

Then Grandma said, "Billy, it'd be the same reason that the stars are brighter over the farm than anywhere else."

I looked up at the darkening sky, and the stars really were brighter. I hadn't noticed that before, and I said so.

"Maybe you need t' practice yer seein', too," Grandpa said. When he said it, he didn't look at me. He just kept staring forward, toward the woods that lay beyond the road.

In the dark, you couldn't see the old dirt road from the porch unless the moon was near full. You could still see the woods in the distance, but the road was invisible, unless a car or truck passed along with its lights turned up to bright.

Even after dark, the comings and goings of country folk on the road continued. Although you couldn't see the cars and pickup trucks from the porch, you could tell how fast they were going by the sound of their motors. Grandma knew the sound of every car and truck motor in the farming community. She could listen and say, "That'd be Aunt Sallie on her way t' choir practice down at church." And then she'd listen some more. After a few minutes, another car would go down the road. "That'd be Frank in his old pickup, takin' dinner up t' old Miz Agent. I gotta hand it t' him, he takes good care of her since her fall." She'd pause, rock a couple of times, and continue. "Sees that she gets a hot meal every night, he does."

Eventually the noise from the road petered out, and for a while, we all listened to the crickets. The only other sound was the creaking of the cane chairs as we rocked back and forth. Then another car passed with a high-pitched whine, and Grandma said, "JP's gonna have t' get that transmission fixed or the engine's gonna drop clean through its mounts."

"Yep," Grandpa said, "that's a fact." But that was all he said. He had moved up to the edge of his seat, with his hands cupped behind his ears, and was listening as intently as he could.

I had first noticed that Grandpa sometimes cupped his hands behind his ears the very first day we were at the farm that summer. I'd asked my dad about it that same night, and he told me then that Grandpa was blind in one eye and deaf in one ear.

"You see," Dad said, "when he was seventeen years old, your grandpa was clearing brush in the pasture up next to the tree-line. He took an axe to a thorn tree, and the tree swung right back at him and buried a long thorn deep in his eye."

"They took Grandpa to an eye doctor in town. But in those days, technology wasn't what it is today. All the good doctor could do was extract the thorn. Your grandpa would be blind in one eye for the rest of his life."

I hadn't known about Grandpa's handicaps, and that caused me to wonder how, being old and handicapped, he was able to hear and see better than the rest of us. I asked Dad, "Which eye is he blind in?"

Dad chuckled and said, "The funny thing is, I was never able to figure that out."

I couldn't stop wondering which was Grandpa's blind eye. The next day, I checked, and Dad was right: I couldn't tell just by looking into his eyes. So, the day after I had talked to Dad, I asked Grandpa.

"Grandpa, Dad says that you're blind in one eye."

Grandpa shrugged. "I can see you just fine."

"C'mon, Grandpa. Which eye is the blind eye?"

He didn't say anything, but pointed to his right eye.

Now, I thought Grandpa might be trying to trick me, assuming that if I knew which was his blind eye, I might try to get away with something and get myself in trouble. Since he had pointed to his right eye, I figured that he must actually be blind in his left eye. So I went to working out how I could test my theory.

In the morning after breakfast the next day, as Grandpa and I walked down the road along the fence line, I tried to test his vision. I got up on his left side, thinking he couldn't see me, and tried to put my hands on the barbed wire fence, to see if I could stretch the middle wire up and the bottom wire down far enough for me to get through.

Grandpa caught me before I could even reach for the wire. So I figured he hadn't been trying to trick me after all, and his right eye really was the blind one.

But since Dad had said that no one had ever been able to figure out which eye was blind, I still wasn't sure. So that same afternoon, I asked again—and this time, Grandpa pointed to his left eye.

Now I was lost. I couldn't be sure if Grandpa was really blind in his left eye, or if he was just playing a trick on me.

The morning after the left eye experiment, Grandpa and I were walking out the front gate from the farmhouse, heading up to the cornfield to see if the tassels were turning yet, when I spotted the old rooster. For years, I had hated that old rooster. He got up on his fence post outside my window at daybreak every morning and woke me up before I was finished sleeping. So I walked up behind Grandpa on his right, a step out of his side vision. I pulled my slingshot out of my back pocket and took dead aim at the rooster as he wandered around the yard.

But before I could pull the sling, Grandpa reached back, took hold of my arm, and squeezed it tight, until I dropped the slingshot on the ground.

"Grandpa," I said, rubbing my arm, "which eye did you say was your blind eye?"

"I can see you just fine," he said again, this time putting the emphasis on the "you." And that was that.

The matter of Grandpa's deafness was no easier puzzle. According to my dad, Grandpa had suffered a series of serious ear infections when he was a boy, and they hadn't had antibiotics back then like they do now. So Grandpa had grown up deaf in one ear. Only he didn't act like he was deaf in one ear—and just like with his eyes, I couldn't figure out which one was his bad ear.

One day, I asked him a question, speaking in a soft voice near his left ear. He heard me perfectly, so I figured the bad ear had to be his right ear. But guess what? You guessed it. He seemed to hear just fine out of his right ear too.

Grandpa was blind in one eye and deaf in one ear, but I could never figure out which. I didn't know if I was ever going to understand him. He was a mystery in so many ways. Despite his handicaps, nothing much got past him. Grandpa could hear and see better than any man I ever knew—certainly better than I ever could. He proved it to us that night as we sat on the porch listening to the night sounds.

On this particular night, Grandpa had some unfinished business, which was why he was listening so hard. The night before, a raccoon had gotten into the henhouse and ravaged several nests, breaking the eggs, putting a fright into the chickens, and injuring one of the smaller hens. He'd done all this harm before Grandpa could get outside and fire the shotgun, which frightened the 'coon away. But we all knew that he'd be back, now that he'd found a way in. Raccoons were smart. This was why a raccoon getting into the henhouse was a situation calling for an immediate remedy.

Grandpa owned three hound dogs that he kept in a pen behind the house. Earlier that night, on account of the 'coon, Grandpa had let the dogs loose to hunt in the dark. I'd stayed on the porch with Mom and Dad and Grandma when Grandpa unleashed the dogs. I didn't want to be too close—even though I was nine years old, going on ten, I was afraid of them. I'd been bitten on the leg a couple of times by a dog when I was trying to deliver newspapers back home, and I'd had to go the doctor for a tetanus shot. Now the one thing I feared more than dogs were shots.

When Grandpa had come around the side of the house and taken his place on the porch, I said, "Grandpa, how is it that the hounds can hunt in the dark? They can't see, and the sounds of the crickets and frogs are so loud, they can't hear."

"They mostly hunt with their noses," he said.

That struck me as strange. My nose was useless for hunting down anything. Sometimes in the early morning, when I was still half-asleep, I could barely find my way to the kitchen, even with the smell of bacon so strong you could taste it two rooms away.

"Their noses?" I said.

"Yep," he said. "Those dogs can smell the trail of a raccoon near half-mile away, even when you"—meaning me—"couldn't smell a 'coon if'n it was right under yer nose."

He moved forward to the edge of his rocker, looking in the direction of the hunting hounds' yelps, and laughed with one of his one-heave-of-the-belly, breathy sort of laughs. The laugh faded fast into a curious smile, and his eyes sparkled. "They see with their noses," he said, with a smile lingering in his voice.

Now Grandpa sat patiently on the porch, totally focused, hands behind his ears as he listened to the dogs hunting in the nearby forest up on the ridge across the road from the house. The dogs never made much noise in the woods—until they got on the trail of some varmint. At first, I couldn't hear them at all, though I thought Grandpa might. He always seemed to hear things the rest of us couldn't hear or see. But, once they got on the trail of their prey, we could all hear them, yelping and barking as they ran through the forest. One minute they were on the left, a half-mile up toward Aunt Tee-Dee's place. Then they ran back through the woods across the road from the house and turned north toward the Baker farm, three-quarters of a mile up the road.

Even when I could hear the hounds, I had no idea what their baying and barking meant. But Grandpa could hear the dogs even when they were a long way off, and he could tell you what they were doing and exactly where they were. Their yelps and barks and howls and yaps sent signals to Grandpa, and he took it all in just like the big Philco radio, picking up invisible signals out of the air. I didn't know how he made sense of it. For someone who was supposed to be blind in one eye, and deaf in one ear, Grandpa sure noticed and understood a lot. I figured he must have a nose like a hound dog.

All of a sudden, Grandpa sat up straight as an arrow. The dogs had started making a sharp, baying kind of bark. Grandpa eased forward in his cane rocker, elbows on his knees, picking up the hound signals, his nose thrust forward as if he was one of the pack. He seemed ready to leap right out of his rocker.

"Well, dag-nabbit! I do believe they're gonna tree that old 'coon!" he said, slapping the armrest on the rocker, as if he could hardly believe they had managed it on the first night he'd let them pick up the scent.

I stopped rocking. "Grandpa, how d'you know it's a raccoon?"

"Don't you hear 'um?" he said.

"Well, yeah, but they're a long way off. How do you know it's a raccoon?"

"'Cause it is," he said.

"But Grandpa, it's dark."

"You be knowin' that smallish elm tree a hundred yards into the woods, the one you used t' climb, back of the old barn?"

"No," I said. I didn't know which tree he was talking about.

"Well, those hounds are chasin' that 'coon up into the gap between Hayes Hill and Little Hill right now, and when they catch him, they'll tree him up that same elm tree."

"Come on, Grandpa. How can you tell all that? You're stone-deaf in one ear," I said

"Who told you that?" He seemed aggravated that I'd brought it up.

"C'mon," he said, and he stood up and took me by the hand. He was determined to prove to me that he could hear just fine. "C'mon out with me t' where they've treed that 'coon, so's you can see him fer yerself."

"Can I, Grandpa, really?"

"Yep, but you gotta stay close t' Grandpa."

So we got our walking sticks, Grandpa got the lantern fired up, and we started downhill on the rocky drive toward the road. Grandpa carried his single-shot 16-gauge Winchester shotgun, pointed downward with the breach open, so you could see there wasn't a shell in it.

"Lēgie," Grandma called after us, "you take care of that boy. D'you hear me?"

Grandpa didn't answer. He just lifted the lantern higher and swung it from side to side, as a sort of signal that he had heard her, and to let her know that he had everything in hand.

I was scared. I'd never been hunting before. It was darker than pitch, and I wasn't sure I ought to be out at night like this. The dogs had quit howling. I couldn't hear them at all. But even without their barking, Grandpa acted as if he knew exactly where they were, and headed straight for them.

As we walked up the old Rock Spring Road in the dark, Grandpa said, "Billy, did you know there are different kinds of huntin' dogs? Regular huntin' hounds can't catch a 'coon. They aren't smart enough by half. You have t' be usin' a 'coon hound. A raccoon can outsmart most any other kinda dog, but he can't outsmart a 'coon hound. A 'coon hound is a very special hound."

"What makes 'coon hounds smarter than regular hounds?" I asked. I got the feeling Grandpa might have noticed how nervous I was, and was trying to make me feel better by distracting me.

"Well, a 'coon hound knows the tricks that a 'coon plays t' try t' get out of a trap."

I expected Grandpa to go on telling me about the special hounds, but he didn't. I waited, but he just left the story hanging there. So I had to pry an explanation out of him.

"What sorts of tricks does a 'coon play on a regular hound that he can't play on a 'coon hound, Grandpa?"

"Well, when a 'coon knows that dogs have got his scent, he runs from 'um, leavin' a clear path fer their noses t' follow. Then he'll climb a tree with long branches…" Grandpa stretched his arms out wide.

I waited for him to go on—but there was nothing else. He just stopped. Sometimes Grandpa did this with his stories. It was his way of making me think. Anyway, he stopped. So I had to crank him up again. He was drawing me deeper and deeper into the story.

"Grandpa, why long branches?"

It seemed as if he had been waiting for me to ask. "Well, the old 'coon, see, he climbs up the tree, runs way out on a limb, and then he jumps as far as he's able, out away from the tree. He lands in the brush, and off he takes."

Again, I thought he would keep going, but he didn't. By then, I'd guessed that he was playing some sort of game with me, but I didn't know what it was.

"Why would he jump back down to the ground, Grandpa?"

"T' fool the hounds," he said. And he stopped again.

Finally, I caught on. Grandpa was climbing that tree with his story as if he was a 'coon, then being completely quiet while I tried to catch up to him. And when I did, he was running the story out on a limb, trying to trick me. Then, when I found him out, he'd jump the story way out away from me again, making me try to follow him.

Grandpa was trying to see if I was smarter than a 'coon hound. I had just finished third grade, so I wasn't sure myself—I had never hunted 'coon before. But I played along. Maybe this was some sort of initiation.

"Okay. How would jumping off the limb fool the hounds, Grandpa?"

He started up again. "A normal hound would sniff his way up t' the trunk of the tree, thinkin' he'd treed the varmint. He wouldn't think t' go out from the tree and sniff a wide circle 'round it, t' see if the 'coon had jumped. So the 'coon would jump off and get clean away, while the hounds stand there, bayin' up an empty tree.

"Now, a 'coon hound knows better'n a regular hound what a 'coon can do, so as soon as he gets t' the tree that a 'coon's climbed, he sniffs it. When he smells it, he leaves a couple of dogs at the base of the tree, and goes way out beyond the longest branches. Then he starts sniffin' a complete circle 'round the tree t' see if'n he can pick up a scent. If'n he does, he calls the other hounds, and they're off on the trail again, bayin' and yelpin' as they chase the 'coon deeper into the woods.

"Pretty smart fellers, huh?" he said.

"Yeah," I said. And I wondered if I had caught my 'coon.

Around this time, we reached the old barn. We crossed the small stream behind it and walked uphill to the upper forty, where the corn was taller than my head. Then we walked about a hundred yards down a long row of cornstalks and into the woods.

As we entered the timberline, Grandpa held the lantern higher and took me by the hand. We walked carefully, so we wouldn't trip over exposed roots or run into a thorn tree. After all, I thought, if Grandpa were to get a thorn in his good eye, he would be able to see so well that we wouldn't need to go into the woods at all. He'd just stare the 'coon down from a hundred yards away, and it would drop out of the tree from being seen to death.

We were just about a hundred yards into the woods when suddenly, the hounds started baying again. They sensed Grandpa coming. We changed our path a little, following the sound of the dogs, and then suddenly, we stumbled onto them circling the base of a tree. Their tails wagged hard in the lantern light, their houndish enthusiasm showing how proud they were to present Grandpa with his prize.

Grandpa raised his lantern a little higher and silently pointed. Up in an elm tree, illuminated in the glow of the lantern, were two tiny red lights—raccoon eyes—looking back at us. The raccoon was exactly where he'd said it would be.

Suddenly, the 'coon jumped up to a higher branch, looking scared to death. He knew he was cornered.

"Billy, hold the lantern up high," Grandpa said in a whisper as he handed it to me.

I was only 4'6", and couldn't hold the lantern up much past five feet—but it must've been high enough.

What happened next came on quickly, and I wasn't ready. Grandpa put one shell in the breach of the shotgun, hefted the gun up, and took aim. It was so dark, and it all happened so fast, I couldn't see which shoulder held the stock of the shotgun, nor which eye he used to take aim.

I saw fire belch out of the barrel of the gun, and there was a sharp crack, louder than any crack I'd ever heard. The crack of a shotgun sounds so much louder at night, when the forest is dark and quiet. I jumped at the sound, jerking my head away from the blast, and almost dropped the lantern.

Suddenly, all the critters in the forest went dead still. Even the dogs were still. But the sound of the shotgun seemed to go on and on, echoing from Little Hill to Hayes Hill and back again.

Something fell out of the tree and landed with a thud in a pile of twisted brush and leaves ten feet from the base of the tree. It sounded real heavy when it hit the ground.

Grandpa didn't hesitate. He moved straight to the spot. He lifted something dark up high, and walked back toward me so I could see it in the lantern light. When I saw it, I wished I hadn't.

Half an hour later, Grandpa and I came walking up the drive: Grandpa holding the dead raccoon by the tail; the dogs right on his heels, jumping to try to get their teeth into the kill; and me, carrying the lantern as high as I could—which by then was just about four feet up. I was getting real tired.

The rest of the family had gone to bed. Amos and Andy and the rest had all visited the big radio box and gone home. Only Dad was still up, waiting for me. When he saw us, he smiled, and I wondered if he had been out with Grandpa hunting at night when he was a boy, and our journey brought back memories for him.

I knew right then that this night would become a memory for me too—it was that extraordinary. Somehow, Grandpa had known from nearly a mile away the exact tree where the dogs had treed the 'coon. He'd heard it with a deaf ear, aimed the gun with a blind eye, and now he had his trophy. The varmint that had caused so much ruckus in the henhouse, stealing eggs in the middle of the night, had been put down for good. But what amazed me most was that Grandpa had been stalking him all along, just by rocking on the porch and using his noticing skills as he listened to the dogs hunt from a long way off in the night.

The hunt for the raccoon ended up being more excitement than I had bargained for. My receptors were worn out, and I needed my sleep. As I shuffled inside, stumbling up the steps of the porch past the big Philco radio, I suddenly realized that everything had its own receptors. The radio had electric receptors that made it possible for it to pick up signals in the air all the way from Nashville. Grandma had tuned her hearing so that she could receive the sounds of car and truck motors. The dogs had receptors in their noses. And Grandpa, with only one good eye and one good ear, could "recept" much more than the rest of us, almost as if he had developed a sort of sixth sense. I guessed that maybe if I got used to listening to the quiet, and listened real deep like he did, even if I had just one good ear, I might be able hear the way he did—things I never thought I could hear. Once, only a few days earlier, Grandpa had told me, "If'n you put yer ear near the ground and be quiet enough, you can hear the grass growin." At the time, I'd thought he must be joshing me—but with Grandpa, you never could tell.

That night on the porch, Grandpa began teaching me to notice. He was teaching me to be fully aware of the present moment, not only aware of the things my eyes could see and my ears hear, but also the things that were unseen and unheard. Sometimes what was unseen and unheard proved to be as important as what could be heard and seen with two good eyes and two good ears.

One day, not long after that night on the front porch, I asked Grandpa, "Grandpa, is listening real deep and being still kind of like praying? I mean, if you're real still and real quiet, like you're supposed to be when you pray, can you hear God whisper to you sort of in your heart, or in your mind's ear?"

"Wha' d'you think?" he said.

I couldn't say. I had never managed to be still enough to hear God whisper to me. "I think learning to pray takes a lot of practice, listening in the quiet for God to talk to you," I said.

"Guess it does," Grandpa said.

I figured that God must say a lot to Grandpa, 'cause Grandpa could listen in the quiet better than anyone I ever knew.

Later, I found myself wishing Grandpa had talked to me more about God. He didn't often answer my questions about religion. It wasn't his way. He wanted me to hunt down the answers by myself, like a 'coon hound trying to tree its prey. But Grandpa did teach me that when you've really practiced your noticing for a lot of years and learned to listen and be real alert in the silence, you may be able to hear what he called the Extra-ordinariness, with a capital "E"—by which he meant God speaking to you.

As the years have passed, I've tried to make time to sit in the evening and be as still as I can, just listening to the night and waiting for God to whisper something to my heart. And I've found that once again, Grandpa was right. Occasionally, when I've gotten real still, been real quiet, and waited on God to speak, I've heard unbidden thoughts rise up into my mind from somewhere inside me—thoughts I knew I hadn't thought for myself.

Whenever I feel out of practice praying, and feel as if God has stopped speaking to me, I try to get my heart real quiet—because sometimes, God will run out on a limb in the dark and jump away as far as He can, just to see how serious you are about keeping on with the hunt. And I have found that if you keep on seeking, and really want to hear, God will speak to you in His own time, and in His own way.

I hadn't expected I would, but even now, I long for those quiet moments spent rocking on the porch in the peace of the evening, listening to stories about the family. I miss that much more than those old radio programs I thought I loved so much.

Now, It's Your Turn:

_____

_____

_____

_____

_____

_____

_____

_____

_____

_____

_____

_____

_____

_____

_____

_____

_____

_____

_____

_____

_____

_____

_____

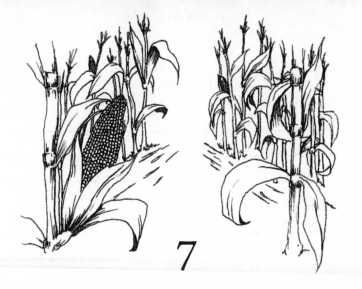

7

The Shearin' 'n' the Shoein': Part One
The Shearin'

Wisdom from the Farm:

Big has a responsibility t' Small. Big needs t' always be noticin' Small and makin' itself a little smaller'n itself, so that Small feels bigger'n it usually feels about itself. Most of the time Small doesn't know its own gift. Small needs someone who knows Small better'n Small knows itself. When Big gets smaller, Small may begin t' recognize its gift. Even then, sometimes, Small can't give its gift 'til Big gets outta Small's way.

G randpa kept about thirty head of sheep on his farm. Of all the animals on the farm, I liked sheep the least. They were always dirty, and they smelled bad. A whiff of a wet sheep was a stench I just couldn't quite get used to.

Maybe the sheep sensed they were undesirable, because they usually stayed to themselves, huddled on one hillside or another like outcasts who didn't belong. I kind of felt sorry for them, but I was glad I never saw too much of them.

In spite of my distaste for them, the sheep were the first animals I worked with. The cows, draft horses, and hogs were all too big. They could accidentally step on my foot, kick me, or bite. Grandpa said that if one of the large animals stepped on my foot, it could easily break a bone.

But none of these dangers seemed to apply to the sheep. They were the most docile of all the farm animals: they didn't kick or bite, and if a full-grown ewe stepped on your foot, she might leave a good bruise, but she wouldn't likely break a bone. The only problem with working with the sheep was that they would scatter in the presence of a stranger—especially a small boy who couldn't stand still. So, even though I wasn't in any danger around the sheep, Grandpa didn't let me work with them until I was ten, and I'd learned to stand still and not make sudden motions.

The first lesson to learn was how to gather the sheep into the sheepfold for the night. At night, sheep are easy prey for wild dogs, and they had to be gathered into pens to keep them safe. We had to account for every sheep to be sure that one hadn't been left out on the farm—but it's hard to count sheep when they are on a hillside. They are in constant motion, and tend to huddle together, so it's easy to count one sheep twice or even three times. Once we'd gotten them in the pen for the night, they were easier to count.

But getting the sheep into the pen was no easy job, even for Grandpa. Sheep are followers. You could get out ahead of them and lead almost all the sheep into the pen—except the last one. More often than not, you had to drive the last one, the one Grandpa called the "straggler."

Late one spring evening, as it was getting dark, I tagged along and watched Grandpa drive the last sheep into the pen down beside the barn. On this evening, Grandpa was having a hard time with the straggler. Every time the last sheep saw him closing on her from behind, she'd look back at him and miss the doorway. Then she'd circle around in a little trot, with Grandpa chasing after her.

I stood on the hillside above the sheep pen watching Grandpa work with the straggler. It was taking forever, and I was getting bored.

"Grandpa," I called out, "why are sheep so dumb?"

"They'd be smarter'n you think. They're just too dumb t' know that they're smart," he said, with some frustration in his voice. He was lining her up for another run at it.

Finally, as Grandpa made another pass at the pen, he faked coming up on the sheep's right side, then intentionally spooked her. She ran to get away from him, and found herself in the pen by accident. Grandpa had outsmarted her.

"Grandpa, why doesn't she know that you're tryin' to help her?"

Grandpa closed the gate on the sheep pen and went to counting to be sure they were all there. "Well, sheep think they're not very important. They mostly feel small and useless. You hear the weak cry they make, that bleatin' sound?"

"Yeah, Grandpa. What're they saying?"

"Well, in sheep talk, they're sayin', 'We feel small.' And 'cause they're small, they're 'fraid of the other animals. They'd be feelin' all defenseless 'cause they don't have strong snouts like the hogs, or nubby horns fer buttin' heads like the goats, or long legs t' kick with like the cows and horses. So, they feel unimportant.

"It'd be a good lesson fer you, Billy, 'bout Big and Small."

"I know, Grandpa; big is better than small."

"Nope. Not hardly," he said. "A lotta good folks make that mistake. I don't want you thinkin' that way."

I was confused. "What way?" I said.

"Well, you might be thinkin' of it like this. You might think that Small owes everythin' t' Big, but that's not right. Be closer t' the truth if'n you understand that Big has a responsibility fer Small. Big needs t' always be noticin' Small and makin' itself a little smaller, so that Small feels bigger'n it usually feels 'bout itself."

We were leaning over the wooden side boards of the sheep pen, looking at the sheep, when Grandpa said, "Billy, unless Big becomes smaller fer the sake of Small, Small can never give its big gift t' the world."

With all this talk of Big being smaller for the sake of Small and Small feeling bigger because of Big, I was beginning to feel a little dizziness in my head. Grandpa was talking in circles, and I couldn't keep up, but there was one question I needed to ask before the dizzy got the best of me. "What gift do sheep have to give to the world?"

"Well, I'm just 'bout t' tell you. Most of the time, Small doesn't know its own gift. Small needs someone big t' take notice of it, someone who knows Small better'n Small knows itself. When Big gets smaller, Small suddenly recognizes Small's gift. Even then, sometimes, Small can't give its gift 'til Big gets outta Small's way."

Now the dizziness was coming on fast. I was beginning to feel a little faint, so I hurried him along. "Yeah, Grandpa, but what gift do sheep have to give?"

"They give their fleece."

"What's 'fleece'?" I said, wondering if he meant their fur.

"Fleece? Fleece is the sheep's fur."

Wow, I thought, *I got it right.* I felt smarter than I knew I was, just being able to answer one of my own questions.

Grandpa said, "Okay, so, d'you understand the lesson 'bout Big and Small?"

"Aaaah, yeah. I guess."

"No guessin''bout it. Billy, this lesson is more important than most folks think. If Big stays Big and ignores Small and Small never gets t' give its gift, the world eventually stops workin' like it's s'posed t', and the farm stops workin' like it's s'posed t.'"

"Grandpa, do you mean that when you take the fur off the sheep's back, even though it's dirty and stinks, the sheep begins to feel more important, like it has something good to give to the farm? You mean it feels a little bigger, right?"

"Yep! That'd be 'bout it. One day next week, Jake the draft horse will teach you the rest of the lesson."

"There's more?"

"Yep! There'd be more. I told you that 'Big and Small's' not as simple as it sounds."

Suddenly, Grandpa changed the subject. "Billy, did you notice that the tulip poplar trees just started bloomin'?"

"They did?"

"Yep, they did! And when the tulip poplar blooms, that's nature's sign that it'd be time t' get our gift from the sheep. So early tomorrow mornin', we're gonna start trimmin' the wool from the sheep's backs. It'd be called 'shearin.'"

I noticed that Grandpa had just said "we." On the farm, whenever Grandpa said "we," that usually included me. I just hoped Grandpa wouldn't ask me to do something too hard.

We left the sheep in their pen and walked uphill to the farmhouse for a late dinner. Afterward, while there was still some sunlight left, I asked my dad to point out a tulip poplar tree so I'd know what one looked like.

Dad walked me just south of the farmhouse where a couple of trees stood, covered with bright yellow blossoms. He caught a low-hanging branch and pulled it down so I could see the blossom up close.

"Bill, look at this," he said. He pointed inside the blossom. "The blossom has six yellow petals, sort of like the blossom of a tulip flower, and about two-thirds of the way to the stem, there's an orange circle. Do you see?"

"Yeah, I see."

"The tulip poplar tree is one of first flowering trees to bloom in the spring. One single blossom seems small, but when you look at the whole tree—" He stepped back and looked up at the tree, which must have been thirty feet tall. "—there are hundreds and hundreds of blossoms, and all those blossoms put together send a loud message. They shout at your grandpa, and all together they say, 'Lēgie, it's time to shear the sheep.'"

"How did Grandpa learn about the message?" I asked.

"I don't know for sure," Dad said. "But over the years, your grandpa has listened closely to the soil, the trees, the weather, and the animals. They talk to him and tell him all their secrets."

The sun was setting, and twilight was coming on fast, so we headed back to the farmhouse and got ready for bed. I had a hard time going to sleep that night. I was too excited. Tomorrow, I would finally graduate to working with the larger animals. But I was also a little nervous about this new adventure with Grandpa, thinking about how small I was to be doing such a big job. I was afraid he might ask me to do something I wasn't prepared to do, like hold one of the sheep while he sheared. I was only ten, and I came up a little short in the area of confidence. But I thought if I had some advance notice, I could muster up my courage to do whatever Grandpa asked me to do.

Morning came sooner than I expected. Before breakfast, we went into the barn, and Grandpa began to lay out burlap bags for packing the wool. I told him what I was thinking.

"Grandpa, it scares me some to have to do something I wasn't expecting to have to do."

"Wha' d'you mean?" he said.

"Like when you didn't tell me in advance that you wanted me to milk the Jersey, and she kicked me off the stool."

"How much advance warnin' d'you need?"

"I don't know. I guess about a week," I said, and stopped a minute to think about it. "Yeah, about a week I think. A week would give me time to get my gumption up." "Gumption" was one of Grandma's words.

"Would, would it?" he said. He turned and looked me in the eye, "A week!" he repeated to himself. He rubbed the bristles on his cheek. They made a rough scratching sound. Even after Grandpa shaved, there was always stubble left, like the debris left in the field from last year's harvest.

"Yer gumption comes up kinda slow, don't it?" he said.

I couldn't think of anything to say to that, so I just stood there, waiting.

"Okay," he agreed. And I was happy we'd gotten that issue out of the way.

After breakfast, I walked out onto the front porch. Grandpa was sitting on the top step, cutting lengths of soft paper twine with his pocketknife.

"What kind of string is that, Grandpa?"

"Well, Billy, after we shear the sheep, we need t' bale the fleece, so's we can get it off t' market. This here be a special twine that we're gonna use t' tie the wool into bales fer when we carry it into town. It's a soft string that holds the fleece in place without tearin' it."

He stood up and started down the steps, passing the lengths of twine to me to hold. And off we went, downhill to the pens.

I trailed along behind, feeling a little afraid. I had no idea how to get the wool off a sheep's back. I'd never seen it done, and I felt a little nervous about it. I was afraid the "we" time was coming soon, and as usual, my gumption wasn't up for it.

A wooden runway ran eight or ten feet from the sheep pen into the side of the barn, with a swinging door to allow access to the corner inside the barn where Grandpa did the shearing. The runway had wooden sides, but no top, so Grandpa could reach over and encourage a reluctant sheep to make its way through the swinging door into the barn. It was a pretty neat setup.

Grandpa took me into the barn to show me the place where he was planning to do the shearing. There, beside the waist-high wooden shelf where Grandpa would lay the sheep on its side for the shearing, was a strange-looking contraption I hadn't noticed before. "Grandpa, what's this thing for?"

"That contraption there'd be a hand-turned shaver. We use it fer shearin' the sheep." There was the "we" again. I was getting more anxious by the minute.

"How's it work?"

"Well, it takes two people workin' together t' operate the shearin' machine. One fella's gotta crank this here handle. See here?" He pointed to a folding metal tube. "When you crank the crank, it turns the tubin', and that powers the shears, so's you can shave the fleece off the sheep. The other fella's gotta hold the sheep and do the shavin'."

I saw a way out. "Grandpa, let me do the cranking part."

"That'd be a good idea," he said. "But once we start shearin' a sheep, you've gotta keep crankin' 'til we finish gettin' all the fleece off that sheep. Don't slow up or stop. D'you think you can manage that?"

"Yeah, Grandpa, I can do it."

When Grandpa had everything laid out just so, he went out and pushed the first sheep in through the door and shut it.

"Billy, while you're crankin', I want you t' watch how the shearin' is done. It doesn't have t' be hard, but there's a right way t' go 'bout it. If'n you don't do it the right way, it'll take you a week t' get all these sheep sheared."

So he set about showing me how it was done. He grabbed the first sheep by the legs and toppled her over on her side. He tied her legs together, front and back, with the soft paper twine. I expected the sheep to fight with Grandpa, like I did when I didn't want to go into the barbershop, pulling back and trying to get free. But once Grandpa had toppled the sheep over onto her side and tied her legs, she lay real still.

Grandpa laid her up on the waist-high shelf, reassuring her by putting weight on her shoulder to hold her firmly as he laid her down. As he did, he spoke to her, strong, but gentle at the same time.

It was magical, the way the farm animals submitted to Grandpa. They seemed to trust him to take care of them. While watching Grandpa with the sheep, I saw Big taking care of Small, Big knowing more about Small than Small knew about itself. Even when he began to put the shears to the sheep's skin, she didn't jump. It was as if she knew she was involved in something important.

"Okay, Billy," he said to me. "Start crankin.'"

The machine wasn't hard to crank, and the cranking made the blades of the shears move like a big electric shaver. Grandpa began shearing the sheep from underneath, and I cranked away as he began.

Now, here was the trick: things had to be done in a certain order. First, Grandpa sheared up the front legs, peeling back the wool as he went. Then he went to the belly and began to clip the wool away, moving up along the sides like he was taking off a wool coat, with the zipper running down the belly of the animal. He sheared fast, and made a few bloody nicks and cuts along the way. That kind of bothered me, but it didn't seem to bother the sheep. I wished that he'd be more careful and work more slowly. He could probably have saved the sheep some small suffering.

"Grandpa, you're cuttin' the sheep," I said. "See those bloody spots?"

He went right on as if he hadn't heard me, shearing away the wool as fast as he could.

"Grandpa, doesn't that hurt the sheep when the shears cut their skin?" I was more than a little bit worried about it.

"Nope," he said. That was all he said. Just "nope."

Considering that I had shared my concern about any pain the sheep might be suffering twice, I was a little surprised that Grandpa didn't get short with me and yell, on account of his temper getting a little strained. But he never got upset with me, not even a little. It wasn't in his nature. There was a calm patience inside my grandpa that told me that he had things under control. You could nick him with a few cutting words, and he'd never flinch. Irritating things could never get to him. In all my life, I never saw Grandpa lose patience with people, not once—not even with me. The sheep felt that calm too, just like all the other animals on the farm.

Grandpa worked so fast that all the wool was off the first sheep in four or five minutes. After shearing a half-dozen sheep, Grandpa said, "Billy, watch close now. I'm wantin' you t' see this, so's you can do this job fer me later."

I watched as Grandpa sheared another sheep, and then another. Once he finished shearing a sheep and had pushed the wool to the side of the stall, Grandpa untied its legs, let the animal get to its feet, and shooed it out the door. It was spring, so it was warming up outside by midmorning, but when the sheared sheep was shoved outdoors, it was shivering from loss of body heat. Steam rose off its back. Sometimes, after the shearing, a sheep didn't want to go outside into the cold, so Grandpa shoved it out, pushing the hind parts. Then he went out to the sheep pen and pushed another sheep inside.

I tried to memorize how Grandpa worked, but I had a tough time concentrating, because the idea of "later" was bothering me. I really didn't want to do this anytime later. I was scared to hold the animal, afraid that it would fight me and get loose. I needed to know exactly how much time "later" meant, so I could work up my courage and be prepared like I'd told him. I wondered if I could make up an excuse.

"Grandpa," I said, "I think I hear Grandma calling me up to the house."

"Yer grandma's walked over the hill t' visit her sister. Can you hear her all the way from there?" He smiled to himself.

He'd called my bluff. "No, sir," I said.

I felt awkward, but that passed quickly when he said to me, "Go over and hold the wool sack open wide and push all the loose wool down t' the end of the bag."

After he had sheared eight or nine sheep and sent them on their shivering way, Grandpa rolled up the wool and tied it with a piece of the paper twine. Then he stuffed the wool into one of the long burlap bags. And then, after the ninth sheep, Grandpa turned toward me and gently took my shoulders.

"Okay, Billy, now I want you t' try. I'll be right here behind you t' help."

I'd had a notion that "later" might be coming sooner than I wanted. "Grandpa, I don't want to do this right now. Remember about the week?"

He acted as if he hadn't heard me. Instead, he brought the next sheep and tied her legs. Then he sat down on a tall stool and positioned the crank so he could turn it with one hand and help me position the animal with the other. Holding her down with one big hand heavy on her shoulder, he handed the shears to me.

My heart felt like it was in my throat, and I stepped away. After seeing the bloody spots where the shears had cut the sheep's skin, I was afraid to try.

Grandpa put his two big hands on my shoulders and moved me close between him and the sheep, so he could reach around me if things got out of control. I didn't want to appear afraid in front of Grandpa, so I took the shears and stood over the sheep with as much confidence as I could muster. Grandpa had chosen a smaller sheep for me to shear. I guess he'd thought a smaller sheep would be less intimidating.

Grandpa rolled the animal over just enough to show its belly. He showed me where to start, and then he began to crank.

The clippers began chattering in my hand. I put my left hand on the sheep's shoulder and felt how still she was. She was so calm, and I had the sense that the sheep was encouraging me to begin the process. It was almost as if she knew she was making a sacrifice in order to contribute something larger than herself to others.

I put the shears on her stomach and began to shave upward along her front leg. The sheep didn't move a muscle, and the fleece came right off in my hand.

I tried to be real careful, but I was cutting the animal right much. She was bleeding some through the cuts on her raw white skin, but I'd made up my mind that I was going to see this thing through, mostly to make Grandpa proud of me. That was always very important to me. I wanted to be as tough and strong as he was.

As I sheared, I discovered an unexpected surprise. I hadn't known sheep's wool was so oily. Before I knew it, my hands were so slippery that I couldn't hold the big shears. Each time I went to trim away the fur, the clippers would shift in my hand, and I would cut the animal sharply. That didn't seem to bother Grandpa, but it bothered me plenty.

"Grandpa, what's all this oil doin' here?"

"Be 'lanolin,'" he said, so fast that I didn't catch it right the first time. So he spelled it out for me: "l-a-n-o-l-i-n."

I was getting dirt and oil and sheep smell all over me. "Grandpa," I said, "is this dirty fur really the sheep's gift to the world?" It didn't seem like it was worth much to me.

"Yep! That'd be her gift t' the world," he said. "Billy, the fleece you're gettin' off this one sheep's back be weighin' 'bout three, maybe four pounds. Once we get it t' market, it goes t' the mill, where the mill workers will clean it up real good and make nearly five thousand yards of worsted wool yarn from it. The wool off this one sheep be worth 'bout $120. Then folks at the mill will gather it up into skeins and sell it t' folks with looms like yer Great-Grandma Barker, who'll weave it into rugs t' keep the floors warm in the farmhouse, and sweaters t' keep folks from gettin' cold in the winter. The sheep's fleece is a gift t' keep the world warm."

"Wow," I said. "I'll bet the sheep doesn't know that."

"Sure she does, 'cause you be showin' her by the way you be holdin' her, and talkin' t' her, and valuin' her gift. She understands better'n you think she does. When we push her back outside, she feels clean and whole, like she's made a difference in this old world."

Soon, I was covered in oil, and a little blood—and I was just finishing the first sheep. I guess it must have taken me fifteen minutes to get this one sheep's "gift to the world" off her back. That may have been a world record for slowness, but it was the best I could do—not having any warning and all.

Finally, Grandpa took the clippers back from me so we could finish the job in one afternoon. I was surprised at how smoothly and quickly he could do it. After we were done, Grandpa loaded all the bags full of wool into the pickup. Later, he would carry the bags of wool to the market.

When I got back up the hill to the house, Grandma had gotten back from her sister's. She took a look at me, and she wasn't too happy with Grandpa. I guess I smelled like a sheep to her—so she decided I would be the next sheep to be sheared.

She threw me in a tub and filled it with hot water. "Too hot!" I told her; but she didn't listen. There wasn't much point in resisting her. I knew that she knew what was best for me, so I let it go, and she went to work getting the sheep off me like I'd tried to get the wool off the sheep. She started with my arms and legs, then moved on to my belly, working her way around to my backside. Then she scrubbed the back of my neck and the top of my head.

As Grandma scrubbed me down, I noticed something that came as a real surprise: I knew what the sheep felt like after they were sheared. Stepping out of the tub, I felt cool and fresh and clean again.

"Sometimes gettin' clean be good fer yer soul." That was what Grandma said. Getting my soul clean made me feel lighter and full of energy.

After that, my views about the sheep changed. I didn't feel so bad for them. They put up with being dirty, isolated, vulnerable, and nicked by shears, all just to give their gift of warmth to the world. They were special animals, and I liked them.

What's more, I had helped the sheep give its gift to the world, and that felt good. Small had discovered its gift and felt proud to give it up willingly. How could I tell? After the sheep had given their wool and gone out into the warm spring air, they ran free, leaping with delight. And after my bath, I felt ready to run and play like the sheep did right after they'd been sheared. That's how I knew.

Once Grandma got me dried off and into some clean clothes, I felt good all over. And as strange as it seemed, I thought I was beginning to understand the animals on the farm the way Grandpa understood them.

Now, It's Your Turn:

_____

_____

_____

_____

_____

_____

_____

_____

_____

_____

_____

_____

_____

_____

_____

_____

_____

_____

_____

_____

_____

_____

8

The Shearin' 'n' the Shoein': Part Two
The Shoein'

Wisdom from the Farm:

Big has a responsibility t' make itself a little smaller, so that Small feels bigger'n it usually feels about itself. Small needs someone big who knows Small better'n Small knows itself. Sometimes Small doesn't know its own gift. When Big gets smaller fer Small's sake, Small can recognize its gift and give it t' the world.

Thursday morning, the week after the Great Shearing, the weather was humid and overcast. Grandpa sat in the wicker rocking chair on the front porch and pulled on his steel-toed boots, lacing them up real tight. Then he went inside, grabbed four bright red apples from the kitchen table, and stuffed them into the big pockets of his overalls. He was out the screen door and on his way downhill, halfway to the barn, before I could get my shoes tied.

He was up to something; I knew it. Every time Grandpa left the farmhouse, an adventure was about to happen.

I ran out the screen door, hollering after him. "Wait for me, Grandpa!"

Below me, I could see that Grandpa had already been into the barn, and was on his way back out. He was leading his giant white Texas draft horse out of the barn, holding the reins in one hand and an apple in the other. I knew that the white horse's name was Jake, but we hadn't been introduced, so I just called him "The Horse."

When I got down to the barnyard, Grandpa had me stand back fifteen or twenty yards from the horse. He said he was fixing to put new shoes on him, and it'd be best if I kept my distance, so I wouldn't spook him.

Grandpa wasn't going to let me do this job. "It'd be right much of a job fer a child," he said. That was fine with me, because even from this distance, I could tell one thing: a full-grown Texas draft horse was huge like a city bus. It was obvious that he could easily hurt someone, even if it was by accident.

Dad told me he had once seen Grandpa shoe a "fractious horse." That's a horse that pulls back and fights you, and can kick you real good. He could break your leg, or worse, even bite. But Grandpa was so big and strong, even the fractious horse seemed calm when Grandpa was around. He seemed to know that no matter how much he resisted, he wasn't going to get Grandpa's goat, so there was nothing else to do but go along with him.

I had never seen Grandpa use big horses to do any of the farm work. So while I was waiting for Grandpa to begin gathering his tools, I asked him, "Grandpa, what's a draft horse do?"

Grandpa shushed me. "I don't call him a draft horse when he's close enough t' be hearin' me, 'cause he doesn't know that he's a draft horse, and it'd get him all confused. Be best if'n you just call him "Jake." That'd be his name, 'Jake.'"

Grandpa told me that a draft horse was good for pulling a heavy wagon, yanking a stubborn stump out of the ground by its roots, or plowing deep into shallow soils with clay and rocks just inches below the surface. He said, "They're real strong animals. But it'd be a funny thing 'bout a horse. Even bein' real big like he be, the tiniest flyin' insects really bother him. So a draft horse isn't as good fer plowin' as a mule."

It seemed odd that the insects pestered both mules and horses, but the mules didn't seem to mind. I figured the mules were just too dumb to pay much attention.

Grandpa told me to stand right where I was, and went back into the barn to gather up the rest of the tools. I thought, *Boy, this would be a great time for Jake to make a run for it,* but the horse just stood there.

Grandpa emerged from the barn with a stool a little taller than a milking stool, and a bunch of tools I hadn't seen before. He had a sharp, curved knife, and a thing he called a rasp, which was a long piece of metal something like a file. He set these tools out on the stool. Then he went back into the barn and carried a heavy anvil out with one hand, and got a big iron hammer, a smaller hammer, and a glass jar full of new horseshoe nails.

While I watched from afar, Grandpa set the stool right close to the horse's right foreleg, sat down, and tapped the horse lightly on his foreleg. The horse lifted his leg and gave Grandpa his hoof, as if he were about to get a shoeshine.

Grandpa used a pair of pliers to pull out the nails that were holding the old shoe in place. He pitched the nails and the old shoe into a big tin bucket and started shaving off the hoof with the sharp knife.

Now, that had to be painful! "Grandpa!" I said. "You're cutting his foot!"

Grandpa didn't say a thing. He just motioned for me to come closer. Then he reached over, got an apple, and gave it to me.

"Give him an apple. He'll be fine."

I crept up to The Horse real slowly, and lifted up the apple as high as I could. I was four feet six inches tall, but the horse's head must have been close to seven feet off the ground, and I couldn't reach that high.

Before I could ask Grandpa what to do, the horse snorted at me, and shook his head from side to side, like he was saying "no." Then he lowered his big head and curled his upper lip at me. *Boy*, I thought, *this horse really needs to see a horse dentist*. And then, just as I was turning my eyes away from the horse's teeth, he took the apple right out of my hand, gentle as could be.

When I turned back to Grandpa, he had finished cutting down the hoof. "Billy," he explained, "what I've just done doesn't hurt the horse any more'n you hurt when you get yer toenails clipped."

"I don't like getting my toenails cut," I said. "Last time, Mom cut one toenail too close, and that toe was sore for a week."

He acted like he hadn't heard me.

"Grandpa, what I am s'posed to do now?"

He didn't answer, so I just stood there with my hands in my pockets, feeling useless. Grandpa took the rasp and began to prepare the sole of the hoof.

"Billy," Grandpa said, "come 'round and look at this hoof."

I walked slowly around the front of the horse and looked. I didn't say anything. I just stood there with my hands still in my pockets, so as not to make any sudden motions that might frighten the horse.

"When you're preparin' the hoof fer a new shoe, you've gotta get out all the gravel and thorns and such that might be stuck in the hoof." Grandpa pointed to a small piece of rock stuck near the center of the horse's bare hoof. "If'n you don't clear that little rock there from his hoof before you put a new shoe over it, it might hobble the horse. That'd be real bad. So, you've gotta make sure that you cut any small rocks or other debris out before you try t' put on the new shoe. Got that?"

"Yes, sir. I got it."

Grandpa picked up the rasp and began filing down the bottom of Jake's right front hoof, so that it was smooth and flat. The rasp didn't make much noise—not like I'd expected. Pretty soon, the hoof was clean and ready to be fitted for a new shoe.

"There's another thing," Grandpa said. "When you go t' shoe a horse, if'n you cut into the 'quick' of the horse's hoof, he'll go lame on you. It's a little like when yer Ma cut yer toenail too close, only worse. That's bad. Don't do that."

I made a mental note not to do that, even though I didn't know what the "quick" was.

Grandpa took a new horseshoe and laid it on the bottom of the hoof to see if the shoe fit, then let the horse put his leg down. The horse just stood there. I thought he might trot off, but he didn't move a single step. It was as if he knew Grandpa wasn't finished yet.

Grandpa handed me another apple and motioned toward the horse. This time, I knew what to do. I stood up on the toes of my sneakers and lifted the apple as high as I could, and the horse lowered his big head and took it right out of my hand.

Then I took a big risk. While the horse's huge head was down picking the apple out of my hand, I tried to reach up and pat him on one of his giant jowls. He didn't like that. He tossed his head up, and his eyes flared open real wide.

"Grandpa!" I cried out. I leapt back so fast I almost tripped. I was scared out of my wits.

Grandpa was working at the anvil, and turned to see what had happened. He figured out right away what I'd done. "Billy, just give him the apple real nice-like. Don't spook him. He doesn't know who you are."

Maybe I spooked the horse, but he'd put a real fright into me. My heart was thumping in my chest, and I started taking short breaths, like I did when I was about to start crying. I was shaking all over.

Grandpa didn't make a move to comfort me. He was more concerned about the horse.

"Billy, see this here horseshoe?" he said. "It'd be a bit too big."

I sniffled quietly from the leftover fright, and didn't say anything. I just watched him.

Grandpa moved over to the iron anvil. He put the horseshoe over the pointy end of the anvil and rotated it, striking the edge of the horseshoe hard to shape the shoe just a bit smaller. The anvil made a sharp ringing sound every time Grandpa hammered.

Grandpa said, "Jake, this small fella here's my grandson."

And the horse turned his head and looked right down at me. No kidding! I was amazed. The horse knew how to speak English!

"Billy, this here's Jake. Say 'howdy.'"

"Howdy," I said. And the horse shook his head up and down a couple times and snorted. It was the first time I'd ever talked to a horse.

"Jake," Grandpa said, "you're big, so I want you t' take good care of my smallish grandson. Always be watchin' out fer him!"

Jake gave a big nod of his huge head and pawed at the ground with his left foreleg.

"Grandpa, can I have another apple for Jake?"

"Nope. You'll spoil him. He doesn't need anythin' from you 'ceptin' yer attention."

Grandpa moved back to the stool, sat down, and tapped Jake's front leg softly. The horse lifted up its leg and gave his foot to Grandpa. It was the darndest thing I ever saw.

Now the shoe fit the bottom of Jake's hoof perfectly, so Grandpa went to driving in the horseshoe nails. He drove those nails all the way into the hoof. It had to hurt something awful. But Jake didn't budge—so I guess it didn't.

Grandpa moved the stool to Jake's other side and went to shoeing the hoof on the left foreleg. That's all there was to shoeing a horse. It didn't seem so hard when I watched Grandpa do it.

After Grandpa finished the shoeing, he put a soft rope halter over Jake's head. A single rope rein hung from it.

"Now we've gotta let Jake try out his new shoes t' see if'n they fit." Grandpa put his two hands on my shoulders, positioning me on Jake's left side, and put the rope in my hand. "Stand right here close by his head, so's he can see you."

I looked up at Jake, and Jake glanced down at me for just a second. Then he turned and looked straight ahead.

"Billy, take the rope and step forward slowly. No need t' be pullin' on the rope; just hold it loose, and don't get more'n a step or so ahead of him. He knows what t' do. Walk him 'round here on this flat ground. Let's see how he likes his new shoes. If'n he's uncomfortable, he'll let us know."

"Grandpa, what if he starts to run?"

"He won't. Just walk slow and stay close beside him, and he'll let you lead him. If'n you need t' stop, just quit walkin', and he'll stop right beside you."

I didn't see how Jake would let me walk him. Standing there beside him, I felt real small next to his hugeness, but I knew Grandpa was right there watching us.

I took one step forward, and Jake lowered his head some and took a step. I stopped, and he stopped. Then I took another step, and he took a step. I stopped, and Jake stopped.

Grandpa was smiling at us. "Go ahead, Billy; walk him."

So I started slowly across the barnyard, walking in a straight line. Jake matched me step for step. But when I got near the fence, I didn't know how to turn him around.

"Billy, just start turnin' yer steps in a circle t' the left. Jake'll take care of you."

I started stepping in a curve away from the fence, and Jake followed me. I was getting the hang of it. It was easy, and slowly, Jake began to make me feel bigger than I was. It was a real good feeling. I could do this thing. I could walk a Texas draft horse.

We walked several circles around the barnyard, and Jake let me lead him wherever I wanted him to go.

"Looks like he feels real good in his new shoes," Grandpa said.

"Yeah," I said. "I think he likes them."

Right then, Jake shook his head up and down, as if to say, "These shoes fit just fine."

After that day, I wanted to go down to the barn and visit with Jake every day. Grandpa always gave me an apple and went with me.

Soon, Jake and I became good friends. He'd taught me how Small could be Big. When someone Big makes you feel important, even though you're small, you start to feel bigger.

Two weeks after we gave Jake new shoes, when the family gathered in the kitchen for supper, Grandma said, "Billy, why're you so skinny? You been swallerin' yer green beans lengthwise?" What she said made me feel real small, and embarrassed that I wasn't bigger, like other boys my age. After dinner, I asked Grandpa if I could go down and see Jake.

"You can go, but don't be goin' into his stall or tryin' t' walk him. You can give him this here apple and talk t' him all you want." And he let me go, all by myself.

I told Jake what Grandma had said, and how it had made me feel small. Jake lowered his head and let me pet his long snout, and I felt important again. Jake was a good listener. And soon, every time I felt small because of what someone said, or because

I couldn't lift the feedbag or raise the water out of the well, I'd get an apple and go to talk to Jake about it.

Talking to Jake made my mind venture a couple years back, to the night the monster storm had hit. That night, the storm had been so fierce, but there hadn't been anybody big to go to who could make us feel bigger.

After breakfast the next morning, I found Grandpa sitting on the front step, sharpening the point on his walking stick. I told him what I'd been thinking.

"Grandpa, do you remember the night of the monster storm, when it rained indoors on us all night?"

"Yep, I remember," he said.

"Well, we all felt small, and there was nobody bigger for us to go talk to. So, who are we supposed to go to when there's nobody bigger than us?"

"Billy, you're forgettin' that the Maker is bigger'n any of us, and He was watchin' over us that night, no matter how small we felt. We could have gone and talked t' Him. And remember that the Maker once made Himself small fer our sakes, so that we could have faith. No matter how small we felt, He'd be there t' help us feel bigger."

Like the sheep, Jake must have thought that Grandpa was the Maker. He trusted Grandpa, and never resisted him. When Grandpa went to put new shoes on Jake, he cooperated. He knew that he needed new shoes. If Jake let Grandpa put them on, as painful as it looked, then Grandpa could use him for more important work than he could if he refused to change shoes. Grandpa said that that was the way we were supposed to be with the Maker; to trust that He knows what's best for us.

The sheep and Jake, they got it; but I didn't get it, not at first. Seeing how Jake and the sheep listened to Grandpa, I began to understand why I had to do things, like wear the new Sunday school shoes that my mom bought for me even though they hurt my feet. Growing up meant that you got your hair cut even if you were afraid of the barber man, and you took a bath every night, even if the water was too hot. It was all meant to benefit me— but more than that, it was a public service. If I didn't resist doing these things, it would make life easier for others. The sheep did what was expected of them, and so did Jake, so I decided that I would, too. Grandpa said that doing such things in a good spirit was called "Responsi-Billy." Later I learned that he was joshing me. He meant "responsibility."

In the end, I was grateful to Jake. He'd taught me that I had a responsibility to take care of those who were smaller than me, and to trust those who were larger. By letting me lead him along, even though I was smaller, he'd taught me that we all had to cooperate with each other on the farm. After all, if anybody felt they could just do what they wanted to do whenever they wanted to do it, the farm would lose its routine and never produce the goods it was meant to produce. And that wouldn't be good for anyone—including Jake, and me, and anyone who, being bigger than someone, might decide one day that it was better to be stubborn than to cooperate for the welfare of everyone else.

Grandpa, Billy, and his new friend Jake

Now, It's Your Turn:

_____

_____

_____

_____

_____

_____

_____

_____

_____

_____

_____

_____

_____

_____

_____

_____

_____

_____

_____

_____

_____

_____

_____

_____

9

The Entrenched Men

Wisdom from the Farm:

You don't have t' play people's games t' be friends with 'um. Sometimes you can be a better friend by stayin' outta their games. One day, when they need a friend the most, they may step outside of the game in search of someone who isn't part of the game, someone who they can talk t', someone who will understand 'um apart from all the silly rules.

Saturday was Market Day in Columbia, and Grandpa and I went every week. Farmers brought their produce from all over the county: baskets overflowing with big red vine-ripened tomatoes, green squash, yellow ears of corn for roasting, and melons good for thumping.

Maury County had some of the richest farmland in America—except Grandpa's farm, which was in the eastern part of the county, in the lower end of the Great Basin, where it was real hard to grow blue-ribbon vegetables like the ones we saw at the market. So Grandpa didn't bring his vegetables to market. In fact, that Saturday morning, Grandpa and I hadn't come to town for the vegetables. We'd come to get a shave and a haircut, two bits—at the same barbershop where I'd gotten my first shave and haircut three years before, when I was eight.

As usual, Grandpa parked his green Chevy pickup on the far side of the square surrounding the Maury County Courthouse. That meant we had to walk past the steps leading up to the courthouse doors as we made our way to the barbershop on the opposite side of the square.

Whenever we took that route to the barbershop, I noticed the same eight or ten farmers sitting on the courthouse steps, talking loudly and waving their hands in the air. They wore weathered jeans, old plaid cotton shirts, and angry faces; and were always pointing their fingers at each other and rolling smokes, or chewing tobacco and spitting into the grass.

The city fathers frowned on their behavior. The men, on the other hand, frowned on the city fathers for making a "no spitting" rule. It was a matter of contention between the councilmen and the men who occupied the courthouse steps. Although that battle of wills never made it to the floor of the city council, most folks in the county knew about the standoff.

I had been coming to the barbershop with Grandpa since I was six, and even now, at eleven, I was still a little afraid of those men. They were "toughs," like the bullies I had run into on the playground back in the city. I always stood a little closer to Grandpa when we had to walk past them.

As we passed, the men on the steps called Grandpa by name. "Mornin', Lēgie!"

They always gave the same greeting, every time we passed by on our way to the barbershop. Grandpa always tipped his hat and replied,

"Mornin', Squirrel, you're lookin' fit. Mornin', Red, how's the wife?" But he never stopped to talk. He just kept walking.

When we had passed the men and were out of earshot, I asked, "Grandpa, how come you never sit on the steps with those men? You know all their names, but you never sit and talk. How come?"

Grandpa looked at me. "Billy, all those men do is sit there all mornin' arguin."

To me, that looked to be about right. Every Saturday the same men were sitting on the same steps, jousting with each other. But for some reason, every Saturday, Grandpa would park on the far side of the courthouse square from the barbershop. Every week, we had to walk past those men, right in the middle of their morning arguing, when we could have avoided them altogether by going around the other way. I was beginning to think that Grandpa took that path to the barbershop on purpose.

In fact, before we left the farm that morning, I'd told my dad that I suspected Grandpa had a plan in mind, parking across the square like he did every time.

Dad had responded, "Billy, I think your grandpa may be trying to teach you a lesson. You're old enough to begin to understand some problems that adults have. Your grandpa knows that those men will be there every Saturday, usually arguing about things like politics or religion. Maybe he wants to teach you that you seldom win an argument with someone when you're talking about politics or religion."

We were almost at the door to the barbershop when I said, "Grandpa, you know a lot about politics and religion. Why don't you talk to those men?"

Grandpa shrugged. "There'd be no point talkin' t' 'um. Every one of 'um has an opinion on just 'bout everythin', and they just sit there all mornin' takin' potshots at each other."

"Grandpa, what's an 'opinion'?"

"Well," he said, "An opinion is when you be thinkin' you know what's right 'bout somethin', and you don't care t' listen t' anyone who doesn't think the way you do."

"Why don't they want to listen to each other?" I said.

"Cause they're 'fraid that what they think is right might turn out t' be wrong, and they can't stand t' be wrong. It makes 'um feel weak t' be wrong."

"But if they're afraid to be wrong about something, how can they ever learn anything new?"

"I think you're on t' somethin' there," he said. "Nope, none of those men sittin' on the steps ever changes his opinion. They just like t' argue."

"Grandpa, why don't you stop and explain it to them?"

"It won't do any good takin' time t' talk t' 'um. They'd be 'entrenched.'"

Grandpa didn't know a lot of big words, and I didn't either, so he surprised me every time he used one. "What's 'entrenched' mean?"

"Well, you see, each of 'um has dug himself a trench. They'd be hunkered down in their trenches, and they won't budge. They'll pop their heads up now and then and take a shot at the other fella, kinda like bandits in a shootout with a rival gang. It's the kinda game that men play when they don't have anythin' better t' do."

I frowned. "I don't like that game. Their shoutin' makes them sound real angry."

"Yeah, when they argue, they do sound mad; but Billy, they're not really angry at each other. They just talk loud. They may have had a pass at some 'corn squeezin's,' and so, they're loud and red in the face. It's part of the game. We just keep walkin', 'cause we're not gonna play those kinds of games."

"Grandpa, what are corn squeezin's?"

"Corn squeezin's? That'd be countrified talk fer 'Tennessee moonshine.'"

I knew what that meant, but I'd never seen my grandpa drink anything stronger than milk.

"Billy," Grandpa assured me, "those men are loud and wave their arms at each other, and sometimes there's a spell of pushin' each another like they was fightin', but they won't hurt you. It's kinda like when an angry dog comes chargin' at you, barkin' real loud with a mean look on his face, and you think he's gonna bite you, but he doesn't. He just likes t' hear himself bark. He'd be a bully, but truth be told, he'd really be the one who's 'fraid of you."

Now, I knew that wasn't right, and I told Grandpa.

"Grandpa, one day last fall I was riding my bike delivering newspapers and this dog comes running into the street right at me, barking real loud, curlin' up his lip, showin' his mean teeth, and he didn't hesitate for a minute. He bit me twice on the leg and tore a hole in my jeans. My mom had to take me to the doctor's to get a tetanus shot."

"Were you in the hospital long?" he said.

"No, Grandpa. I didn't have to go to the hospital. It was just a dog bite."

"So it hurt fer a minute, but you got over it pretty quick, did you?"

"Yeah, pretty quick," I said. Grandpa was taking some of the heat out of my thinking.

"Well, Billy, these men are like the dog that doesn't bite. They won't hurt you no matter how mad they seem, okay?"

"Okay," I said.

I thought for a minute. Then I asked, "Grandpa, are those men your friends?"

"Yep! I'd say we'd be friends. I've been knowin' those men fer years and years. I just don't stop t' talk t' 'um. Come along now, we've gotta get a shave and a haircut."

Afterward, Grandpa took me across the square to the Woolworth store, where a teenage boy was sweeping the unfinished wooden floors with a long-handled push broom.

The boy held the door open for us. "Mornin', Mr. Lēgie."

As we entered the store, Grandpa replied, "Thanks, Tommy. How's yer mom?"

"Ma's doin' real good now that the shingles have left her."

"That's good t' hear, Tommy. Be sure t' tell her that I asked about her."

"I will, Mr. Lēgie, I will." And we went over to sit on the stools at the soda counter, where we each got a chocolate ice-cream soda.

Everywhere we went—the courthouse, the bank, the barbershop, the co-op—people knew my grandpa. If we walked down Main Street, most of the folks we passed knew Grandpa, and he knew them. I never could figure out how he made so many friends. He was a man who never said many words, and living so far out in the country, he seldom socialized with people. He only had one really close friend his whole life, and that was his brother Calvin. But, up and down the streets, people called out, "Hey, Lēgie," like he was the best friend they ever had. I think it may have been because he wasn't an entrenched man, and respected other people's opinions.

While we were at Woolworth's, I bought some comic books to keep me from getting bored on the farm during the long afternoon siestas. But, when we left the store and began walking back to the truck, my curiosity got the better of me. "Grandpa," I said, "how come everyone knows you? You never stop and talk to folks."

He didn't answer. He just tipped his hat to old Mrs. Derryberry, who was walking by, and said, "Hello, Fanny. How's Jack doin' up at the University?"

"Hi, Lēgie," she said. "Thanks for asking. Jack's doing very well. He just can't decide what he wants to be when he grows up, an accountant or a banker like his pa."

Grandpa smiled at her. "Oh, he'll figure it out before long." Then he tipped his hat, and we moved on.

It was nearly noon as we approached the courthouse on the way back to the truck. Those same men were still camped out on the steps, ready to go to war with each other in their "game." This time, Grandpa took off his hat and smiled, and called each one by name. He said, "I want you t' meet my grandson, Billy;" and he told me to wave. So I did.

One of the men said, "Lēgie, looks like you've got a mighty fine young man there."

Grandpa just nodded and put his hat back on his head. As we continued on our way to the truck, I noticed that I didn't feel as intimidated as I had when we'd passed by the entrenched men earlier.

That day, I learned the lesson Grandpa was trying to teach me: you can be friends with people without having to play their games. If what they do isn't productive, just say "hi," ask about the wife and children, and keep on going. Don't let a loud, angry voice get in the way of what you're doing. It's just a part of the games that people play. Some folks are getting nothing done and going nowhere all the time. And time's all you've got.

One day, years later, it dawned on me that if one of those men were to get himself into real trouble and needed a real friend, he might get up off the courthouse steps and walk alongside Grandpa to the barbershop and say, "Lēgie, I need t' talk t' you 'bout somethin', and you're 'bout the only one I can trust."

When you really need help, because you've become "entrenched" in one opinion or another, or in one situation or another, if you won't get up out of your trench, no one can really help you. And if you've already dug your trench too deep, it may be too late already. Still, I think Grandpa would intentionally walk by to speak to you, no matter how deep a trench you'd dug.

When we got to the truck, I asked Grandpa if we could go by the Piggly Wiggly before we started home. "Yep, I 'spect that'll be okay," he said. Holding his hat on his head with his right hand as he opened the truck door with the left, he ducked to fit himself into the driver's seat. The old truck groaned as it gathered in his weight, and we were off to the grocery store.

At the store we bought a couple of crates of Nehi soda, half grape and half orange. We always got some orange and some grape. Sometimes my brother, Rick, and I argued about which was better. I liked the grape best, but he liked the orange. We didn't get angry at each other about it, we just didn't agree. We both had our own opinions, and sometimes I guess we got a little "entrenched" about them.

Now, It's Your Turn:

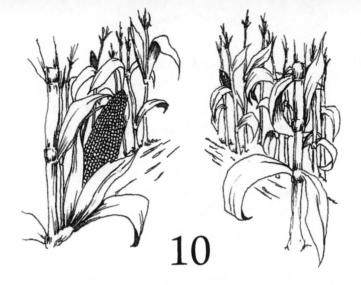

10

The Rogue Bull Meets His Match

Wisdom from the Farm:

"Being-Watched-Over" is a very special feelin'. Someone is always watchin' over us, whether we know it or not. Even if'n we do somethin' bad in the pitch black, someone is watchin'. If'n you can get past the discomfort of that truth and get used t' the comfort that that feelin' brings, it'll deliver you in more ways'n you can possibly imagine.

Two hundred yards downhill from the farmhouse stood the old barn. Its wooden siding, now gray with age, once sat horizontally edge to edge, just right; but now the old boards had grown askew. Some of them, having fought and lost their battle with the rusted nails that could no longer hold them, had splintered and were pulling back, making the walls warp outward. The old barn made a great planetarium: at night, you could close all the doors, sit inside on a bale of hay, and watch the stars through the cracks.

The whole structure leaned toward the roadway, ten degrees from the vertical, like an old man leaning hard on one crutch to keep from falling. Because of the tilt, the barn doors no longer fit—so when Grandpa left them open, it made a tunnel through the length of the barn.

On the far end of the barn, the tunnel opened into a scrub field of wild grasses, thistles, and bluebells. That field was off-limits, because that was the field where the old bull lived.

Grandpa intended to keep that bull as far away from his grandchildren as possible. He had fenced the field off thoroughly with stout posts and tightly stretched barbed wire, which made for a pretty secure fence. The only passage out was through the entire length of the old barn. There were one hundred-twenty feet of hay bales, empty feedbags, horseshoes on hooks, and assorted rusty tools that separated the bull from freedom.

By late July of 1955, I was eleven, invincible in my mind and generally full of myself, prone to playing the typical pranks some young boys play at that age. The gate down near the barn was made of wooden slats, and I had climbed onto it to sit and watch the old jet-black bull, who was fifty yards away. I had a rock in my hand, but I knew I couldn't hit him at that distance, so I was tossing it from one hand to another, waiting to see if he would come any closer.

Grandpa had warned me about the bull. He'd told me the bull was a rogue. I wasn't sure what that meant, but I was pretty sure the old bull was dangerous.

I had a question I wanted to ask, so I climbed down from the fence and walked around to the front of the barn, where Grandpa was hanging up the harnesses he'd used on the mules that morning when he had done some plowing in the upper field.

"Grandpa, what made the old bull so mean?"

He didn't look up from what he was doing, but he'd heard me. "Grandma thinks he was born mean," he said. "But he wasn't."

"How'd it happen?" I said.

"Well, over the years, older boys who'd be havin' a little mean in 'um too would walk down this rutted dirt road past this field on their way t' school, peltin' the bull with rocks. I reckon their meanness just kinda rubbed off on him."

I dropped the rock I'd been juggling, so Grandpa wouldn't see what I'd been thinking.

"How mean is he, Grandpa?"

"Sometimes he gets so mad that he'll break right through the barbed wire, and I'll have t' go hunt him down and start repairin' the fence."

"Would he be mean at me?"

"Mean is mean."

"Boy, somebody could get hurt," I said.

"Yeah. I oughta run him into town and sell him t' the folks who can take the "mean" outta him permanent. That way he'd finally be worth somethin'. He's not much use 'round here anymore."

"Grandpa, will he break through the fence if he sees me?"

I had seen the bull eyeing me, and there was enough meanness in his stare to put the fright bone-deep into a slightly uppity, occasionally prankish boy like me.

"Might," said Grandpa. "Anytime he spots a young boy, his bullish blood boils. So, Billy, listen t' me, like I've told you before, and don't ever go near that field. You hear me, son? That old bull will charge at you fer no good reason, and he'd be eighteen hundred pounds of hamburger on the hoof."

Oh, great! I thought. Another nightmare trying to come to life in my sleep. I still dreamed occasionally about dinosaurs. For years I had been tracking them down, hunting around the farm for their fossilized bones. So now, along with dinosaurs in the cornfield, the wild buffalo roaming in the grassland, and the giant sloths in the vegetable patch, there was a raging rogue bull in the scrub field in back of the barn wanting to come visit me in my sleep!

Grandpa carried the harnesses into the barn and hung them on hooks attached to ropes. When he pulled on the ropes, they lifted the harness off the dirt floor of the barn so that they hung from a wooden beam overhead.

"Don't be worryin' 'bout the bull," Grandpa said. "He's not likely gonna take on the barbed wire just t' get t' you. Let's get up t' the farmhouse. Grandma's probably got dinner waitin' fer us."

The next morning, Grandpa had some chores to do, and he told me I could come along. After breakfast, we walked down to the barn. Grandpa sat down on a three-legged milking stool at the front of the barn. While he started fixing the thin copper spraying rod on a big pump-handled insecticide sprayer, I commenced throwing rocks at a rusted old tin can I'd set up on a fence post as a target. I was careful to stay on the far side of the barn, away from the old bull.

Grandpa was intent on his work, facing toward me, but not looking at me. The full length of the barn lay open behind him, and the old bull spotted me from fifty yards away.

That day became the first day of the rest of my life. My old life died of fear, and my new life was born of relief, rising up right out of the dust.

I was pelting that old tin can with rocks. The bull must have seen the motion of my arm, heard the plink as the rock struck home, and seen the can when it jumped off the fence post. He quickly put it all together in his bullish mind, his blood driving up the pressure in his boiler belly.

Because I was near that field, I kept an eye on that bull, so when he noticed me, I stopped throwing the rocks and watched him. I could tell that he intended to get to me if he could. He waited a few seconds, building up a bullish head of steam, and then he charged.

Out of the field he came, down a slight incline, making the turn through the barn toward me. I saw him coming and froze on the spot. My throat closed up tight, so I couldn't even shout to Grandpa. I opened my mouth and tried: "Grrr...an..."—but I couldn't get it out. Grandpa, who was hard of hearing in one ear, had no way of knowing that the bull was coming, churning up the turf and mud at full speed.

His "Meanness-on-the-Hoof" turned the corner and skidded on the mud, his forward motion briefly throwing him off his stride. He regained his footing as he entered the alcove that ran through the barn. His massive head was lowered as he took dead aim at me, eyes bloodshot and froth around his muzzle. I was a goner.

He was kicking up a dust storm as he passed midway through the barn. Grandpa sat, completely absorbed as he cleaned the copper rod of the sprayer. As far as he knew, nothing out of the ordinary was going on. The bull was closing fast on him from behind. It was clear from the bull's course that he intended to pass Grandpa, break out into the open, and grind me into the ground. I was about to pay the ultimate price for the sins of other rock-throwing boys not unlike myself, and I started repeating the Lord's Prayer. I said it so fast, I skipped right over "And forgive us our trespasses" and rushed on to "and deliver us from evil," hoping I wasn't about to see the "Thy kingdom come" part suddenly come for me.

All I remembered later was a blinding flash of copper in the sunlight. Grandpa moved so fast he was a blur. Without even looking, he whipped that metal tube to the side and hit the bull square on the muzzle so hard I heard the ring in his nose chime. That old bull came to a stop right in his tracks, stunned by the force of the blow he hadn't seen coming. Then Grandpa, who had known what was happening all along, stood up and hit that bull hard in the head with a board, turning him around. Then he kicked him in the rump, and shouted at him as he chased him back through the barn into the field.

After folding the far doors of the barn together and securing them with a chain, Grandpa came walking out into the morning sunlight toward me. I was afraid he would kick me in the rump too, and chase me up the hill to the farmhouse with the bent copper rod in his hand. By the time he reached me, tears were rolling down my dust-covered face, and I was shaking like a scarecrow in a strong gust of wind.

Grandpa put his huge hands on my shoulders and turned me hard toward the house. He didn't wipe my tears or have me blow my nose into his bandanna, like Grandma would have. And he didn't say a word as we trudged up to the house. Not one word. Sometimes "no words" has a more powerful effect than a torrent of angry words.

When we got to the farmhouse, Grandma took one look at me and said, "Now, what have we got here?"

She got a wet washcloth and cleaned my face. "What happened, Lēgie?" she said.

Grandpa held up the bent copper tube and said, "Tomorrow, I'm takin' that old bull t' town and settin' him on a train t' the slaughterhouse."

Now I felt sorry for the old bull. Go figure! I just couldn't imagine them grinding him up on my account. But the next day came, and Grandpa didn't take him. I guess he still had some use for him there on the farm after all. Maybe as a reminder to his grandson that he had better listen good to what his grandpa said to him.

Two days later, early in the morning, I was with Grandpa up on the tree line, checking the traps he had set out the night before to catch a clever red fox that had been causing havoc in the henhouse. We came to one of those traps, and it must have seemed like a good time to make his point.

Grandpa tripped the trap and it snapped shut. He pushed it out of the way. Then he knelt down on his knees in front of me and took his hat off. As he rubbed the sweat off his nearly bald head with his oversized handkerchief, he said, "Wha'd I tell you about the bull, Billy?"

I could feel the tears begin welling up inside me. The one thing that could hurt me more than any other punishment was to be a disappointment to my grandpa. "I know what you told me, Grandpa, but I guess I need to listen better to what you say, and take it more seriously."

I guess that was the right answer. He took me gently by the shoulders and laughed that short, deep, hoarse laugh of his.

"I'd be guessin' that'll teach you somethin', won't it?"

"Yeah," I said, sniffing away a couple of tears that had almost gotten to the surface.

And then he said something I didn't understand until many years later. He said, "Don't be forgettin' yer deliverances, son. Don't ever forget yer deliverances."

Grandpa never told Grandma exactly what had happened, and he didn't tell my mom and dad. It was between us men—or at least between a man and his smallish grandson.

Apparently, the lesson took. I think I've noted every deliverance since, every one of them an act of grace that I didn't merit. If you really pay attention to all those deliverances with thanksgiving in your heart, it sometimes seems like there's been a great, loving Presence watching over you, with a copper spraying rod in one hand. I knew that Someone Up There had his eye on me, protecting me from myself and other out-of-control things.

Once, I mentioned to Grandma how that feeling felt—the feeling of knowing that Grandpa was watching. She called it the "bein'-watched-over" feeling. And to this day, as I write this page, I still remember the day that I was delivered from "the valley of the shadow of death" by a bear of a man who seemed to know everything that was happening on that farm every second, even when I thought he wasn't looking. I had been delivered by my grandpa, wielding the Rod of Moses attached to the nozzle of an insecticide sprayer, and it was the first time I understood what "being watched over" really meant.

Now, It's Your Turn:

_____

_____

_____

_____

_____

_____

_____

_____

_____

_____

_____

_____

_____

_____

_____

_____

_____

_____

_____

_____

_____

_____

_____

11

The Miracle of the Walking Stick

Wisdom from the Farm:

When you be wounded, it'd be better t' be held tight by someone strong, even when it hurts t' be held. Bein' held tight means that yer healin' doesn't depend on yer own strength. It means that there's someone stronger'n you takin' care of you. You don't cause yer healin'. You submit t' the healin', and bein' held tight is part of the healin' process.

Take any long, inch-thick straight stick lying on the ground in the woods, then peel the bark off and rub down the bare wood with oil to seal the pores. Now cut the stick to a length of five feet, and wrap some coarse tape around the thickest end to make a handle. Then whittle the other end to a dull point, and you have one of the most versatile farm implements ever devised by man—the walking stick.

I had watched my grandpa make himself a new walking stick just this way. He used it for just about everything. If we came across a black snake in our path, Grandpa would pick it up on the end of the stick and flip it aside into the brush. If we came to a barbed wire fence and needed to cross over it into another field, he'd wedge the walking stick under the top wire and push it up while he stepped down on the middle wire with his boot. He'd knock a ripe apple off the top limb of an apple tree with it, hold aside a bramble bush that lay across our path to let me pass, even redirect an obstinate cow back toward the barn by tapping its flank. He'd knock down a hornet's nest (don't try this at home) while staying back a safe distance, and clear away the cobwebs that the spiders wove up in the corners of the front porch and in the barn, up where the rafters met the vertical beams.

A good walking stick was as beneficial to a farmer as a Swiss Army knife was to a Boy Scout master. Its uses were endless. Whenever Grandpa walked the fence lines or surveyed the farm to find things that needed fixing, he carried his walking stick. Whenever I went out on the farm with Grandpa, and he carried his walking stick, I carried mine too. Grandpa had made walking sticks for me and my brother Rick, and now that I was eleven years old, I was learning to use my walking stick the same way Grandpa used his.

There was something magical about a walking stick. Having mine with me made me feel stronger somehow. Every time I took it out onto the farm, I found a new use for it. My walking stick helped me tame small parts of the farm that were becoming wild—and as Grandpa told me, to tame any small part of the farm was one step in the work of managing the whole land.

Among its many uses, a walking stick had one special use, which I considered the best use possible. In the right hands, a walking stick can be used to set things free—and as it turned out, one day, we really needed it. On that day, Grandpa's old walking stick saved a life.

It was early morning, about a week after Grandpa had saved me from the rogue bull. We were up in the woods on the ridge line, checking the trap that Grandpa had set to snare the red fox that had been scavenging the henhouse. We'd lost three hens the night the fox broke in, and by now, Grandpa had been trying to trap him for over a week.

Grandpa was using a "jaws of death" type trap: two half-circles of steel with long, sharp teeth on one edge, and hinged together by a powerful spring. If some animal stepped into the middle of the trap, the spring would snap the two half-circles closed, snaring the victim as sure as if it had got its leg caught in the jaws of a shark. It was an ugly thing to look at, and seeing what it did to the victim was worse.

That day, the trap had finally snared a victim—only it wasn't the elusive red fox. There among the trees just below the ridgeline, lying on her side among last season's leaves, was a smallish sheep not much bigger than a lamb. She had gotten loose from the flock overnight, and lost in the dark, stepped into the trap. Her left hind leg had been crushed, and she was bleeding badly.

Grandpa stepped on the trap's spring release with his boot—but for some reason, it didn't release. It was stuck.

Without the spring release, we were in trouble. We tried to get near the sheep, but our approach spooked her, and she lurched away from us. With every effort she made to escape the jaws of the trap, the vicious teeth dug deeper into her leg. No matter the pain, she still fought to be free.

I hated that trap. It wasn't fair. "Grandpa," I said, "what're we going to do?"

"We're gonna slip up on her real slow-like, and hold her tight so's she stops strugglin' some."

"We?" I said.

"Yep! I'm gonna need yer help with her."

"Grandpa, I don't want to," I protested.

But he didn't pay any attention to me. "Now," he said, "I need you t' put yer arm 'round her neck so's her head's behind yer back." He grabbed me around the neck, giving me a firsthand lesson in how he wanted me to do it.

So I grabbed her around the neck. Once I got hold of her, I discovered she was bigger than I'd thought. She struggled against me so hard, I thought I wouldn't be able to hold her.

Finally, when I had her neck secure under my left arm, Grandpa said, "Now, Billy, you gotta use both hands. Be grabbin' her front legs and slowly pullin' 'um out from under her, while I be liftin' the trap off the ground."

I grabbed her legs and held on tight.

"Grandpa, I can't hold her," I said. I was gripping her forelegs while the trap had a painful grip on her back leg. She was fighting with all her strength to get free. But just about the moment I was going to lose my grip, she went slack in my arms. Every few seconds, she would arch her back and jerk away, but she had lost most of her strength, and began to lay still.

"Okay, now be holdin' her tight. Don't be worried 'bout hurtin' her. It'd be important to her that you hold her real tight."

I widened my stance, setting my feet firmly on the ground, and tightened my hold a bit more. Grandpa thought fast. He hadn't brought his heavy leather work gloves with him, and being cautious not to get his hands caught in the trap, he wedged the small end of his walking stick between the jaws of the trap, forcing it in as far as it would go. Then, holding one of the jaws of the trap to the ground with his boot, he pushed up on the walking stick just hard enough to open the jaws wide enough to free her hind leg.

"Okay, now lift her foot outta the trap."

I was afraid to touch the sheep's crushed leg. I knew it would hurt her. But I had learned on the farm that sometimes you have to hurt worse before you can hurt less. So I took hold of her leg—and she kicked away from me, cutting the badly damaged leg again on the exposed teeth of the trap. Her whole body suddenly lurched, knocking me over backward. She almost got away from me: I had run out of arms and legs to hold her.

"Billy, you're gonna have t' get a firm hold on that leg!" Grandpa said.

Grandpa could have done this easily without me, I thought. I really didn't want to grab the bloody leg. I was caught in the "frozen-with-fear" trap, in almost as much panic as the sheep. Grandpa was going to have to get me loose mentally before I could help get her loose physically.

"Son!" Grandpa said firmly. He didn't holler at me, just looked me directly in the eye and spoke in a stern voice. "Grab her leg!"

Finally, I reached down and grabbed the sheep's leg, and Grandpa pried the trap open a little further. Out came the leg, bloodied and trembling in my hand. She immediately fought me, struggling, trying to stand up.

"Hold her down, Billy," Grandpa said. "Don't let her move. If'n you do, she'll struggle against you, and if'n she gets loose, she'll try t' stand, and we don't want her puttin' any weight on that injured leg. Lie down and pin her shoulder t' the ground so's she can't get up. Put all yer weight on top of her!"

Grandpa pulled the walking stick out of the jaws of the trap, and they closed with a snap, a scary metal-on-metal clank. He leaned the walking stick against a tree, and moved the trap out of the way, along with the chain that anchored it to the ground. The sheep lay in a bed of old leaves, quivering, with me on top of her. The walking stick had set her free.

But I couldn't celebrate yet. The sheep was squirming underneath my weight, shaking like she had a high fever. I was afraid she was going to get away from me!

Grandpa leaned down to us. I was half panicking, using all my energy to do what he'd told me and keep the sheep from moving, but he was utterly calm. "Okay, Billy. Get up off her now so's she can breathe, and place yer two hands on her shoulder. You don't have t' hold her anywhere but at the shoulder. Pin her shoulder down tight, and she won't fight you."

Grandpa showed me how to pin her shoulder to the ground. He talked to the sheep softly, and she let him hold her broken leg without struggling against him. I was surprised how still she became when she couldn't move. I could see why local farmers brought their sick animals to Grandpa.

Grandpa took out his bandanna and tore it in two pieces. He bound the sheep's front legs together with one piece, and her back legs with the other. She lay on her side, panting, but she was still.

"Okay now, Billy, I'm gonna pick her up and lift her over yer shoulders. Hold her feet in front of you with both hands, like this."

He showed me how to position my hands. But at eleven years old, I was slight for my age, and didn't weigh more than seventy pounds. Even though the sheep wasn't much more than a lamb, she had to weigh close to fifty pounds. I was outmatched, and I knew it.

"Grandpa, I can't."

He didn't say anythin' like "Yep, you can"—not a word of encouragement. He just lifted the sheep and put her across my shoulders.

"Let's be carryin' her back t' the house," he said.

I started to walk with the sheep across my shoulders, but I hadn't gone ten steps before I felt her legs begin to slip out of my grasp. I bent forward, trying to hold her weight on my back while I got a fresh grip.

"Grandpa, help! She's too heavy!"

Grandpa lifted her off my back. He put her on the ground, then picked her up, setting her over his shoulders. As he held her in his strong grasp, she seemed to relax. Sometimes holding someone tight is better than holding them too loose.

The farm animals all seemed to relax when they felt Grandpa's strength. When I asked him about it, he said, "Billy, that's how it be with God. Once you be knowin' God's strength, you can relax into it some."

We carried the sheep back to the house—or rather, Grandpa carried her back to the house. When we reached home, Grandpa laid the sheep down in the grass and began to work on her leg. It was badly broken, and I could see the bone and tendon glistening white in the sunlight.

I expected Grandpa to find a way to put her out of her misery quickly, like horsemen did when horses were injured this badly. I'd seen him do that sort of thing himself, mercifully putting some creature out of its misery without a second thought. Grandpa could be real tough and efficient about life and death on the farm.

But he surprised me this time. Instead of dispatching her, he took a tube of ointment out of a box that Grandma had brought from the house. He very gently rubbed the soothing ointment onto the sheep's broken leg. After straightening the leg bone, he put the leg into a short splint, and wrapped it real tight.

While he worked on the broken leg, Grandpa said, "Billy, that's what a sheep gets fer wanderin' away from the flock!"

I was still nervous for the sheep. "Grandpa, will she be okay?"

"We'll see," he said. There was no false optimism in his voice. Nature would take care of the rest—or not. Either way, he'd done all he could.

After he finished with the sheep, Grandpa walked me back out to where that ugly trap sat. Midday was coming on quick, warm and humid, but it was cooler up among the trees on the ridgeline. The trap lay sprung shut where we'd left it.

I expected Grandpa to yank the spike that secured the trap right out of the ground, but he didn't. He wedged his walking stick between the teeth and pried them open again, reset the trap, and covered it with leaves.

After all we had just been through, I couldn't believe it. "Grandpa! What if another sheep gets caught?"

"Won't!" he said. "We'll count 'um careful tonight t' be sure we have 'um all in the pen."

"Yeah, but something's gonna get caught," I said.

He didn't say anything. He must have felt he didn't need to explain it to me—and he didn't. Still, I hated that trap.

Later, as we rocked on the porch, Grandpa told everybody how I'd gotten the sheep's leg out of the trap and carried it all the way home, which was stretching the truth so far it was almost out of joint. That night, I went to sleep thankful that we had Grandpa and his walking stick on the farm, taking care of us and all the rest of the creatures.

Early the next morning, we went out to check the trap again. I was real relieved to see that there was nothing caught in it, but a couple mornings later, Grandpa finally caught the red fox. Before I knew what he was doing, he took his walking stick, and with one well-placed blow to the head, dispatched the fox for good.

Grandpa skinned the red fox and kept the pelt. He knew a man in town who'd buy it from him for ten bucks.

I thought that if it had been me who had found the fox and had to decide its fate, I would have brought the fox home like we had the sheep, and bound its wounds. At the age of eleven, I was getting old enough to ask why. Why was the sheep nursed back to health, while the fox had to give up his life?

But even though I didn't understand why one had lived and the other died, I knew that Grandpa was lord of the farm. I was just the grandson. Grandpa always seemed to know best, and I trusted him to decide what was right.

In the end, I decided that some questions weren't meant to be answered. Puzzling over them didn't help, and eventually, I learned to make peace with them. I held that troubling question tight—but I let myself stop fretting over it. Like the sheep, I let it be, and trusted the One who holds us tight to deal with the answer.

But I knew one thing for sure—it's better to be the sheep and listen to the shepherd, than to be the fox who tries to outsmart him.

A walking stick can help set things free. There were many things that wanted to defeat the farm: weeds that sprang up in the garden, broken fences, rocks that settled in such a way as to dam up the stream, and trees that fell across the path. I began to see how these sorts of things and others kept the farm from growing, and I learned to use my walking stick and other sources of leverage to set the farm free.

Maybe the most important thing I learned was that I was caught in the trap of feeling sorry for myself. I always felt too small to try, and too ashamed of not being strong enough, to do a big job. At times like these, my walking stick made me feel stronger and helped set me free from myself.

Now, It's Your Turn:

_____

_____

_____

_____

_____

_____

_____

_____

_____

_____

_____

_____

_____

_____

_____

_____

_____

_____

_____

_____

_____

_____

_____

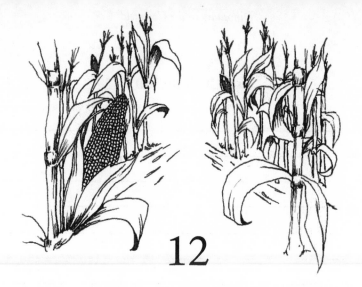

12

The Carpenter's Pencil

Wisdom from the Farm:

The Maker be leavin' marks all over His creation. They'd be called "meaning-added marks". When you search fer 'um with all yer heart, you'll be findin' um everywhere you look. And when you start t' findin' 'um, you start t' understand Him. His plan fer yer life be written all over you, and over all of His creation.

By the time I was twelve years old, I had used all kinds of pens and pencils in school, so I knew what a pencil was supposed to look like—yellow and roundish, with a pink eraser on the end. But the pencil that Grandpa carried around the farm was like no pencil I had ever seen. It was green, and it was flat.

I first started paying attention to Grandpa's pencil one Friday in July of my sixth-grade year. Grandpa and I were sitting on the front step of the farmhouse getting ready to go out and walk the farm, when he pulled his pencil out of the breast pocket of his Duck Head denim overalls and began to sharpen it with his penknife.

I sat quietly, watching him work. My first thought was that a pencil like that wouldn't fit into any mechanical pencil sharpener I'd ever seen. Using a knife to whittle away at its flatness must be the only way to give it a sharp point. But as Grandpa whittled, I saw that the point he was making was uneven. It wasn't a nice smooth point like the kind I got when I put my pencil in the pencil sharpener at school. *That point is going to break off the first time he uses it,* I thought.

A pencil of that shape must have some special purpose, but I couldn't imagine what it would be. So I asked him.

"Grandpa, what kind of pencil is that?"

"Be called a carpenter's pencil," he said.

"Why is it flat?"

"All carpenter's pencils be flat," he said, as he tried to scrape the lead into a point that would make a good mark.

"Yeah, Grandpa, but why is the pencil flat?"

"Full of questions, aren't you?" he said, with a raspy deep laugh cut short—just one good heave of the chest.

I said, "I've never used a pencil like that. I was just wondering if a carpenter's pencil has a special purpose."

He stopped whittling and glanced at me, then looked down at his weathered hands, which had been nicked and scarred many times by the very penknife he was using to sharpen his pencil. After a thoughtful pause, he looked at me again with a smile and said, his voice full of humor, "The pencil be flat so's you can write on things that be flat."

I had to stop and think about that. Somehow, that didn't seem like the answer I was looking for. That's a funny thing about questions: sometimes, you have to have a hunch about what the right answer might be before you can even ask the question. If the response you get isn't the answer you were expecting, then you can't be sure you've gotten the right answer. It's like wanting to know how a word is spelled and going to the dictionary, only to find that you have to know how to spell the word so you can look it up to see how it's spelled. Once you think you know how to spell the word, you look it up, and then the dictionary tells you how it's really supposed to be spelled.

This never made any sense to me. It was just one of those many mysteries that nobody has ever solved.

"Grandpa, are you sure that's why that pencil is flat?"

"Well," he said, "It'd actually be flat so's it won't roll away from you while you're workin', like a round pencil would."

Now that sounded like a good answer to me, so I figured it must be the right one.

Over the next few days, I watched Grandpa closely. I noticed that every time he took the pencil out to write on something, he licked the lead with his tongue. I couldn't imagine why he did that. There had to be a reason.

"Grandpa, why did you lick the pencil like that?"

"'Cause it helps the lead make a darker line when it'd be wet with spittle," he said.

That sounded right, so I tried to think of another question.

"Grandpa, what's it taste like when you lick it?"

"Well, Billy, it'd be tastin' a good bit like pencil lead." And before I could think of another question, he said, "C'mon. We've got work needs doin.'"

Up he got, and was off, with me following close behind, wishing I had a carpenter's pencil I could use to make marks on things.

As I watched Grandpa that day, I noticed that he made short notes on everything—little marks to remind himself later of what he meant to do. He called them "cyphers." He licked the end of his carpenter's pencil and drew a line across a board, so that when he sawed it, it would be the exact length he needed to replace the splintered board on the side of the chicken coop. When he put out a fresh salt lick for the cows, he wrote the date on a piece of heavy brown wax paper and put it under the block of salt, so he could remember when he'd laid it out. He wrote on the door of a stall in the barn to remind himself of the date that the new calf had been born. He wrote on the wooden slats he used to stake up the tomato plants, so that he would know when he'd planted them.

Some of Grandpa's "cyphers" didn't make sense. They were like a code you couldn't break unless you had the key, and the key was the mysterious way that Grandpa saw the farm. Lots of times, I had to ask what a certain mark meant—like, for example, the big "X" he wrote on the slender trunk of a cedar tree.

Later that morning, as we walked the farm, we passed through a stand of cedar trees about half a mile south of the house. There must have been a couple hundred of them.

Grandpa stopped to study the trees. He felt their bark, and looked up and down the trunks. Then he took out his pencil, licked the lead, and made an "X" on one of the trees.

I couldn't tell what made that tree so special. Confused, I asked, "Grandpa, why'd you put an "X" on that tree?"

He put his big hand on the smooth, paper-like cedar bark, and patted the tree like he was right proud of it. "Looks like every other tree in the stand, don't it?" he said. "But this here tree's been whisperin' t' me, remindin' me that it's late spring, and its sap's just 'bout quit risin'. Can't wait much longer if'n I want t' strip off some of its bark."

"Why would you strip off its bark?" I asked.

"Oh, we'll only peel back the bark in small sections, so's we don't harm the tree. Then we'll soak the peelin's. If'n you use 'um before they're dried, you can wrap 'um 'round a cut on yer hand, arm, or leg, and it'll keep out infection. If'n you dry 'um, you can make rope out of 'um; or you can use 'um t' start fires in the fireplace. The bark makes real good kindlin' fer gettin' yer fire started. We can use it fer all sorts of things—weavin' baskets, and wrappin' things t' keep 'um fresh. So I'll come back t' this tree in a day or two and relieve it of some of its bark."

Now that I knew what Grandpa's "X" meant, I was astonished that such a simple mark could tell you that a tree could be used in so many ways. All I could think was that if I'd come across that tree by myself, I would never have guessed what the "X" on it meant.

And that tree wasn't the last place I saw Grandpa add his marks. Over the course of that day and the next, I paid close attention to him, and saw that he left marks on just about everything. Everywhere marks! He made marks on burlap bags, on the lids of ten-gallon milk cans that he was sending to the dairy, and on the sides of the vertical honeycomb frames in the beehive. He scratched his marks with his penknife on the little metal 'tags' he put in the ears of sheep so he'd know which sheep were his in case a stray from another farm found its way into his flock. He used his pencil to write the names of family members in the family Bible anytime there was a birth, marriage, baptism, or death. The whole farm was covered in Grandpa's marks.

Grandpa also made marks on slips of paper, which he kept in a little spiral notebook that he carried in another of the many pockets of his overalls. He used them to keep records he couldn't keep anywhere else, to write down the number of feet of barbed wire he'd need to repair the fence where the old bull had bolted through it, or how many eggs he was getting each day from the henhouse. At the auction house in Columbia, where they auctioned off all kinds of farm animals, Grandpa used his flat pencil and slips of paper to keep track of the latest bid. If Grandpa ever forgot to carry his notebook, he'd find scraps of paper in the glove compartment of his pickup, or tear away part of a feedbag; or, if we were in town, he'd pick up a napkin from the fountain at the Woolworth store. He'd stuff them into the breast pocket of his overalls. By the end of the day, he'd empty the wad of paper notes he'd collected onto a table in the kitchen and sort them out, as if he were putting together a map of the farm.

On Saturday evening, I told my dad what I'd been doing, how I'd been watching Grandpa write notes all over the farm, and how the "X" on the cedar tree let him know what the tree was good for. Dad listened carefully until I'd finished. Then he said that I ought to think of Grandpa's notes as "meaning-added marks."

Being full of questions, I asked him, "Dad, what are 'meaning-added marks'?"

"Well, Bill, when your grandpa makes a mark on something, that mark tells you something about the thing that the thing couldn't tell you about itself. So if you added up all his 'meaning-added markings' from all over the farm, you'd know something more about the farm than the farm knew about itself."

He'd lost me.

He went on: "And that 'something more' would be what Grandpa understands about the farm. But it would be hard for us to understand, unless we understood Grandpa's plan for the whole farm. Any one of his marks alone only tells you part of a much larger story."

Even though I didn't know Grandpa's plan for the whole farm, the notes Grandpa made still explained a lot to me. It seemed to me that if I went all around the farm, gathering up Grandpa's "meaning-added marks"—his cyphers, his symbols, his digits, and his other tiny notes—I would know just about everything that was happening on the farm. If I brought them all back to the farmhouse and laid them all out on the kitchen table, they'd be like a jigsaw puzzle. Once I got all the pieces to fit together just right, the puzzle would turn out to be a treasure map—one that would lead me to that secret place where Grandpa performed his miracle of turning gray rocks into yellow grain.

I explained this theory to Dad. I could tell he was impressed by my figuring, which made me feel pretty smart. Dad said I was getting to the age that I was able to do some deductive reasoning.

"What's 'detuctive reasoning'?" I asked.

"'Deductive reasoning' is when you take a whole bunch of facts that don't seem to be related to each other, and use them to see a larger picture in which all those facts, taken as a whole, work together and say something about a subject that no one of the facts says alone."

Grandpa came to dinner late that evening, because he had to get the milking done down in the barn. After dinner, I asked him to talk to me about how his marks fit together to make up his plan for the farm. So, before the rest of the family gathered on the front porch for our nightly family time, Grandpa and I walked down to the barn. When we got there, Grandpa sat down on a bale of hay, took out his penknife, and went to whittling a hickory whistle for me. Grandpa always liked to be doing something with his hands while he explained things.

I waited impatiently for him to tell me how his marks worked. Finally, just as I was wondering whether he'd forgotten about my question, he said, "Billy, the thing 'bout the farm is that it thinks it knows a whole lot more 'bout itself than it really does. If I didn't put marks all over the farm, it'd think it was a wild place, and go t' weed and thorn and scrub brush in no time at all. That's why we need farmers. Farmers help a farm become much more'n it could ever be on its own."

I nodded, excited to understand. "I get it, Grandpa. Farmers are real important people because they can read the land and explain to the land all that it might become if all the parts of the farm work together. Is that right?"

"Be somethin' like that," he said.

"The farm needs to be able to do 'abstract thinking,' doesn't it?"

"What?" he said, as if I had spoken to him in a foreign language.

I was about to explain, but he kept going.

"Billy, since we're talkin' 'bout this 'knowin,' there'd be somethin' else you should know. Just like the farm, we be always thinkin' that we know more 'bout ourselves than we really do."

"Think of it like this. There'd be this Farmer in Heaven who has a plan fer all His creation. That includes you and me. He leaves cyphers 'n' marks all over you and yer life, but 'til you've walked all over the "land" that be yer life, and gathered up all the markin's and notes and put 'um all together the way the Farmer intends, you can't know the greater plan fer yer life. You'll just live day after day, passin' the time, not knowin' who you be or where you're goin.' D'you understand that?"

"Yeah, Grandpa, I think I do."

And I did. I know I did, because the next Sunday, I finally understood one of Pastor Pope's sermons. Nothing that Pastor Pope had said in the past had ever made much sense to me— but on that particular Sunday, I understood.

During his sermon, Pastor Pope talked about how God had made each one of us special. But he said we couldn't know how special we truly were, until we understood our 'higher purpose' in God's creation. As the pastor talked, I started to get excited. This sounded almost exactly like what Grandpa and I had been talking about down by the barn!

I sat up in my seat and listened intently to the pastor, as my mind started working double-time. Maybe, if I could find some of the "meaning-added marks" that were written on my life, I would be able to understand why I felt so afraid at times. Maybe I'd be able to figure out why I sometimes felt like I wasn't worth much to anybody. Maybe I could figure out why I wasn't as good at some things as other people were, and why there was something kinda wild lurking inside me, that wanted to get out and do bad stuff. And, if I could read all the "meaning-added marks" that God had made on me, maybe I could even figure out the real reason God gave my life to me.

After we got home from the Meeting and had our lunch, Grandpa took the bag of offerings that had been collected at church and sat at the table under the bedroom window. He pulled out his flat green carpenter's pencil and went to adding up the offering, making marks on a piece of brown paper torn from one of Grandma's Piggly-Wiggly grocery bags, just as he had every Sunday afternoon for over twenty-five years.

Grandpa was very careful when he counted the Lord's money. He gathered little stacks of one hundred pennies, twenty nickels, ten dimes, or four quarters. Each stack made a dollar. Finally, he added them all up, sent a report to the church, and put aside the money to be taken to the bank in town on Monday.

But today, I had a question that couldn't wait for Grandpa to count up the money. So, thinking myself very clever, I came up with a way to get the answer to my question without waiting.

"Grandpa, can I help?"

"Can you stack all these pennies and nickels and dimes in stacks of five?"

"Yeah, Grandpa, that's easy."

While we were counting the Lord's money, I asked Grandpa the question that had been bothering me ever since I'd heard the pastor's sermon. "Grandpa, what happens if I don't know that I have a higher purpose and never read the 'meaning-added marks' in my life? I mean, what if I didn't pay attention? I could miss the meaning of the marks around me and never understand my higher purpose, couldn't I?"

"Yep. Unfortunately, that happens t' some folks."

"What happens if you miss your higher purpose?"

"Well, first thing would be that you'd always think of yerself as just an ordinary person. You'd be thinkin' there's nothin' extra-ordinary 'bout yer life. And if'n you're not lookin' fer the 'meanin'-added marks' in yer life, pretty soon you forget they're there, and quit lookin' fer 'um altogether. Then, just like the farm, if'n you're not careful, yer life can go t' weed and wildness pretty fast. So findin' yer 'meaning-added marks' be important work."

Later that afternoon, after I'd had a nap, I walked out to the pasture to help Grandpa drive the cattle back to the barn. When we'd finished, we milked the Guernseys, and while we were milking, I said, "Grandpa, I think I understand."

"Understand what?"

"Well, listen," I said, feeling pumped. "You know how it is with questions, how you have to have a hunch about what the answer might be in order to tell if the answer you get could possibly be right? Well, it's the same thing. You've got to have a hunch about what you don't know about yourself to be able to tell whether what you think about yourself is really who you are or not." I stopped suddenly, feeling a little bit dizzy from all the explaining I was doing.

At first, Grandpa just looked at me with a real puzzled look on his face, like he didn't have a clue what I was talking about. But then he said something that made me think he did.

"You know, Billy, life's right much of a puzzle, and folks can spend their whole lives and never put the pieces of their lives together. Maybe it would help if'n you thought of yer life as a jigsaw puzzle. You already know the shape of some of the parts of your life. If'n you look at the pieces that you've solved, they'll give you a hint 'bout the shape of the pieces you're still missin'. The Maker not only leaves notes all over yer life, so's that you can gather up most of the pieces; He leaves you hints 'bout the pieces that are still missing. The hints mean that you have t' do some of the work yerself. The Maker isn't gonna do all the work fer you. You have t' work some of the puzzle out fer yerself. When you do this, then you own the final solution, and that "ownin'" helps you value the purpose of yer life even more."

"That's what I just said, Grandpa!"

I was about to explain some more to him, but the sun was beginning to get low in the sky. We had finished the milking, and it was time to head up the hill to the farmhouse for supper.

Before we started home, Grandpa took his carpenter's pencil out of his pocket and made a note on a slip of paper. I didn't know what he'd written, but as I examined all the thoughts I'd just been explaining to Grandpa, I wondered if he'd made a note to remind himself to tell his grandson that 'pride goeth before a fall.' I knew that some of what I had said had been an attempt to show Grandpa just how smart I was becoming, and that could be prideful.

But even though I was getting to that age when I was starting to feel right smart, I still had a lot of questions needing answers. The moment he took out his carpenter's pencil, another one occurred to me, and of course I had to ask him.

"Grandpa, why doesn't that pencil have an eraser?"

He didn't say anything. He just put the pencil away quietly and started walking, heading back up the hill toward the farmhouse, his pencil in his pocket and his grandson three steps behind.

Now, It's Your Turn:

_____

_____

_____

_____

_____

_____

_____

_____

_____

_____

_____

_____

_____

_____

_____

_____

_____

_____

_____

_____

_____

_____

_____

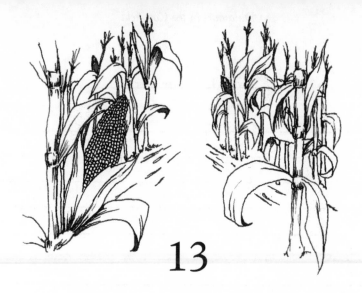

13

The Well, Be More'n a One-Man Job

Wisdom from the Farm:

Don't be goin' off all prideful-like 'bout the things you think you've done, as if you'd done 'um all by yerself. No one ever does anythin' good all by himself. Somewhere down the line, someone has given you a helpin' hand, and you're probably not even aware of it. Their part in yer success needs t' be remembered. It'll be teachin' you humility when you understand that you had help along the way.

"Grandpa," I said, "is that really a well?"

The first time I saw the well on Grandpa's property, I had just turned nine. The well was new since last year, and didn't look like any well I'd ever seen. It was little more than a narrow pipe about ten inches across, sticking straight up out of the rocky ground 150 yards downhill from the house. Little did I know that its sudden appearance would mark the beginning of a struggle that would last until I was twelve years old.

"Yep, it'd be a well alright," Grandpa admitted. "Not much t' look at, I guess."

The well sat among the rocks about thirty yards from the old barn, between the barn and the farmhouse. Grandpa kept it covered with the lid from a ten-gallon milk can. Above the well-pipe were three stout branches, which had been cut from a tree and lashed together at the top like a teepee. The top of the three-legged teepee stood seven or eight feet above the well-pipe. Inside this three-legged structure, hanging just below where the branches were lashed together, hung a large pulley, and over the pulley ran a long, heavy, rusty chain. One end of the chain lay in a big pile on the ground just outside the teepee, and the other was hooked to a slender metal cylinder about five feet long and maybe six or seven inches in diameter. The cylinder was just the right size to fit inside the ten-inch well-pipe.

"It's strange, Grandpa. The wells I've seen are big circles made out of bricks and stones." I circled my arms around in front of me as wide as I could to show him what I meant. "They cover them over with boards sometimes, to keep cats and stuff from falling in.

"That'd be a citified well, like the ones you see as you get closer t' town," he said.

"Who dug this well, Grandpa?"

"I did, last fall," he said.

"How come you didn't build it wider across?"

"No need," he said.

Well, this talk wasn't going anywhere, so I let it go.

As Grandpa took the lid of the milk pail off the pipe, I was struck by a sudden desire to help.

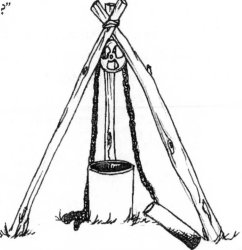

"Grandpa," I said, "let me draw up the water."

"Nope," he said firmly, with a shake of his head. "Drawin' water from the well be too heavy a job fer you. When this here bucket be full of water, it weighs more'n you do even with yer shoes and socks on."

"C'mon, Grandpa, let me try."

"Billy, stubborn isn't gonna get this here water up t' the house."

"Just let me try once."

"Nope," he said again. "But I'll tell you what. You watch as I draw the water, and I'll show you how it works. Then next time, we'll try t' draw the water together. How'd that be?"

"Okay," I said, feeling small and disappointed.

Grandpa began. "First thing we do is take this long metal cylinder and lower it slowly down the well-pipe. This cylinder is gonna be our bucket. Before we put the bucket in the pipe, we need t' be sure that the chain that's attached t' the bucket rides smoothly over the pulley up here." He reached up and adjusted the chain, so that it fit right into the groove in the pulley. Then Grandpa said, "Now, tell me how you'd get the bucket down the well-pipe. Would you just put it inside the pipe and drop it?"

I thought about it for a second. "No. That would probably dent the bucket from it banging against the pipe as it fell," I said. "Might even damage it so bad that it would get wedged in the pipe, and then we couldn't push it down or pull it up."

Grandpa smiled. "You've seen this done before, haven't you?"

I was pretty sure from his tone of voice that he was joshing me, but I answered him anyway. "No, Grandpa. It just seems logical."

"'Logical'? Where'd you learn a five-dollar word like that?"

"Grandpa, I'm in the third grade. We've already learned a bunch of big words."

He smiled, reached out to put his huge hand on top of my head and mussed my hair. I hated it when people did that to me. It made me feel small, but I could tell by his response to my explanation about putting the bucket down the pipe that he was proud of me. Then he said, "Okay then, tell me how you'd do it proper-like."

"I'd hold the chain in one hand, put the bucket into the well-pipe, and lower it a few feet at a time as I let the chain out."

"Would you now?" he said.

"Yeah, Grandpa, that's what I'd do."

"Yup, that'd be 'bout right. But before we lower the bucket down the pipe, let me show you the bottom of this bucket. See, this here bucket has a special butterfly valve on the bottom." He held up the end of the bucket and pointed to the valve. "If'n you're gonna draw water outta this well, you're gonna need t' understand how this here valve works."

"Now," he said, "imagine that this bucket is goin' down the well-pipe, and it strikes water. What, bein' as 'logical' as you are, happens then?"

I said, "The water pushes these two little half-circle doors open, and water fills the bucket from the bottom up."

"And when we start pullin' the bucket full of water up the well, what happens t' the little doors?"

"I guess the water in the bucket forces the two little doors closed, trapping the water inside the bucket."

He looked at me and said, "Did you say you've done this before?"

I could tell he was joshing me again by the hint of a smile on his face.

"Well," he said, "You're a pretty smart young fella. Since you seem t' know how the bucket works, maybe we could pull the water up together."

"Gee, that'd be great, Grandpa!" And I grabbed the bucket from him, carried it over to the well, and started to fit the bucket into the pipe.

"Whoa, there," he said. "Let me help. I'll hold the chain."

We fit the bucket into the well-pipe and began lowering it. Grandpa fed out the chain, and I kept the chain centered in the well-pipe as the bucket slowly went down.

"Grandpa, how far does the bucket have to go before it hits the water?"

"This here well'd be 'bout seventy feet deep. So we've got a lotta chain t' feed out."

When the bucket reached the water level, the chain went slack. I couldn't see or hear the bucket filling, but I could tell by the changing tension on the chain that the little trapdoors had opened at the bottom, letting water rush up into the bucket until it was full. Grandpa and I tugged on the chain to raise the bucket, and the trapdoors at the bottom shut tight, trapping two gallons of water inside.

We were ready to pull the bucket up the well-pipe. "Grandpa, let me try," I insisted again.

"Okay. You pull, and I'll gather the chain as it comes up outta the well. You don't want t' get yer foot tangled in the chain as you raise the bucket."

I pulled the first five feet, and it was easier than I expected. *I can do this*, I thought. *It's really not that heavy.*

Then the bucket cleared the level of water in the well, and the weight of the water in the bucket pulled back against the chain.

"Grandpa!" I shouted. "I can't hold it!"

"I've got it," Grandpa said, grabbing the chain above my head.

I pulled with all my might, but drawing the water up was too hard. Frustrated, I handed the chain to Grandpa. "Sorry, Grandpa. I'm not strong enough."

"You will be one day," he said. "Let me help you."

So Grandpa pulled the chain from the top just below where it came across the pulley. I piled the chain up in a beehive shape on the ground so that we wouldn't get our feet tangled in it, and in this way, we drew the water together.

As Grandpa began to pull up the chain, hand over hand, he said, "Billy, there'd be 'bout twenty-five pounds of water in the bucket, and the bucket itself weighs six pounds. Then there'd be seventy-plus feet of chain addin' another forty or so pounds. Add it up. How much pullin'-down weight is that?"

I tried to think. "I can't do the figuring in my head, Grandpa."

"It'd be over seventy pounds." He continued to pull the chain. It was no great effort for him. "And how much d'you weigh, now that you're nine years old?"

"About fifty-five pounds," I said. I was real skinny—about ten pounds lighter than the average boy my age.

"So the water be stubborn fer you t' draw, 'cause you don't have enough upward-pullin' weight yet t' offset its seventy pounds of downward-pullin' weight," he said. "This year, why don't we put you in charge of lowerin' the bucket down the well, and I'll draw the water and carry it up the hill t' the house? Next year, you can try again."

When the bucket reached the surface, it was soaking wet from the dunking it had taken at the bottom of the well. We lifted it clear of the well-pipe and set it in a large water bucket. Then we pushed on the rod where the chain was hooked to the top, and the trap on the bottom of the metal cylinder sprang open, sending two gallons of fresh water rushing into the new bucket.

"Now remember, Billy," Grandpa said, "gettin' the bucket up outta the well's just half the job. If'n you're gonna be drawin' the water, you've also gotta be carryin' it uphill t' the farmhouse.

Now, cover the well-pipe, and we'll be gettin' this on up t' yer grandma."

There was a 150-foot vertical rise from the level of the well down near the barn up to the farmhouse, so carrying the bucket up the hill was a real hard thing in itself. But Grandpa hefted the bucket easily, and carried it the whole way without a hint of tiredness. I trailed behind him, exhausted from my efforts, wishing I could be as strong as him.

That was how the job of drawing water from the well became, to me, a test of my manhood. I was real impatient to be grown up, and I wanted to prove I was getting stronger by drawing the water the way I'd seen Grandpa do it. But the bucket didn't care about my feelings. There was no compromise with it, no pretending that you were big enough if you weren't. So I had to admit to myself that I wasn't ready, and that I still had a lot of growing up to do.

After that, every summer, I asked Grandpa if I could try to draw the water from the well. The next summer, I was ten years old, and full of confidence. "Grandpa, I'm bigger this year, see?" I said. I showed him the tag on the inside of my t-shirt. It was at least one size larger than the one I'd worn the year before.

He studied me. "How much d'you weigh this year?"

"About sixty pounds," I said.

"Billy, you're not big enough yet."

"Grandpa, let me try," I pleaded.

"Okay, you want t' try? Then lower the bucket."

I lifted the bucket and set one end into the pipe, while Grandpa held the chain. Then I took the chain from him, lowering the bucket down the shaft until I felt the chain go slack. I turned and looked up at Grandpa, waiting for him to tell me what to do next.

"Be lettin' the bucket fill 'til you feel the chain go a little bit heavy in yer hands, but don't let go," he said.

The bucket filled until its weight pulled it deeper into the water, and I could feel the chain tugging downward.

"Okay, Grandpa, I think it's full."

"Lemme feel," he said. He reached over and yanked on the chain. "Yep, it'd be full, alright. Now pull, one hand over the other, like this." He showed me, but by now, I'd seen him do it lots of times. He didn't have to tell me that part.

Just as before, the first five feet were pretty easy, as the bucket was still down in the well water, but as soon as the bucket broke the surface way down below, a sudden downward pull lifted me off my feet.

Grandpa grabbed me before my hands rose far enough to be pinched in the pulley overhead. With half a laugh in his gravelly voice, he called out to me.

"Billy, let go. I've got you." He held the chain in one hand and set me down, his arm around my waist, and looked at me kindly. "How 'bout we try again next year?"

"Yeah, next year, I guess; maybe," I said, unhappy that I had failed. I was in a hurry to grow up, but my efforts were providing a much-unwanted lesson in humility.

Every year, Grandpa would stand me and my brother Rick against the kitchen doorframe, draw a line with a straight edge, then write our age and the year beside the line with that flat pencil he always carried in the pocket of his overalls. Between my tenth and eleventh year, I was sick with a slight bout of polio, and hardly grew at all. Once again, I failed to draw the water. But when I was twelve, I finally hit my growth spurt. The doorframe showed it, and the doorframe never lied. The tag inside my t-shirt was two sizes bigger, and I weighed seventy-two pounds. I'd been trying to pull up the bucket now for two years, but this was the first year that I outweighed the water bucket. Maybe this year, I would succeed.

I asked Grandpa if I could try to wrestle the stubborn water out of the ground on the very first day of our summer visit on the farm, the second Tuesday in July. So, that day, we walked downhill to test my grown-up-ness—and what Grandma called my "stick-to-it-tive-ness," which was one of her favorite words.

It was early morning, and I needed to draw fresh water for breakfast. Grandma was waiting up at the house for us to bring the water so she could start making the biscuits. I felt like the whole farm was watching my performance. I was really pumped to conquer the well this year, and I felt like a gladiator about to enter the Colosseum.

As I got ready to wrestle the chain, I asked Grandpa if I could use a pair of work gloves. My thinking was that if I had a pair of gloves, I could get a better grip, and the wet and rusty chain wouldn't be so slippery. When I asked, Grandpa just smiled, and handed me his gloves.

He had to be joshing me. Grandpa had the hands of a Viking warrior. I put on the gloves and tried to pull the loose chain over the pulley, but I could tell right away that those gloves were going to be more trouble than help. Every time I took hold of the chain, the extra leather from the oversized gloves doubled itself around the chain.

Right then, I had a flashback to my lessons in Sunday school. I remembered the story of King Saul, who gave his armor to David just before he went out to face the giant, Goliath. David was just a scrawny teenager, and the King's armor swallowed him up. He couldn't fight the giant that way. So, inspired by David's example, I gave Grandpa's gloves back to him. You always had to fight your own battles with the strength God gave you.

I lowered the bucket down the well-pipe, playing out the chain as it went down until I felt it go slack, and waited for the bucket to fill.

"Okay. Now pull the chain hand over hand."

"Grandpa, I know," I said, feeling just a little irritated. I knew what I was doing. I'd been trying to do it for years.

"Okay, you can do it." He could see that I had my mind set on it. This was going to be the year.

After the bucket was full, I reached over my head, grabbed the chain with two hands, and pulled down hard, my elbows folding in tight against my sides, my hands coming right down in front of my face, the chain brushing by my cheek. I could feel the seventy pounds of weight pulling against me. It was as if there were four or five elves in a cavern down below, and they were pulling downward hard as they could. They weren't going to help me a bit.

I let go of the chain with my right hand, holding it with my left, and reached high up with my right to grab another handful of the tight-stretched chain. Again I pulled as hard as I could until my hands were in front of my face, and I went down to my knees, allowing all my weight to lift the bucket. I stood, reached up again, caught another grip, and pulled again. I must have been red in the face with trying.

There wasn't any talk between Grandpa and me as I fought the rusty chain. You can't talk and pull water up the well at same time. Childish groans and tight-lipped spewing sounds came out of me as I took deep breaths in and out. The only other sound was the chattering of the chain coming over the pulley. I knew that Grandpa was behind me; I could feel him there, but he didn't say anything. No encouragement was offered.

I took a third handhold and pulled my hands down close to my chest, letting my feet lift up from the ground for a moment so that the chain held my full weight. Then I took a fourth, and slowly came the fifth. I was doing it. Rust from the chain covered my hands, which were beginning to dampen with sweat, making it harder to hold my grip. The only thing going for me was my knowledge that if I could hold on, with every handful of chain

I wrestled up the well-pipe, the total load would become lighter by the weight of a couple of feet of chain. But at the same time, I could feel my strength slipping away from me.

I kept pulling. This was the "Battle of the Bucket," and I fought it in silence. I didn't say a word. Grandpa didn't say a word. All I heard was the sound of the chain falling as Grandpa guided it into a pile clear of my feet, and the squeaky turning of the pulley overhead.

Minutes passed. Each pull of the chain left another rusty mark on my cheek. I kept my head down, my shoulders scrunched up against my neck. I knew that if I looked up to see the chain come over the pulley, I'd lose my grip, and the bucket would fall back down the pipe. The elves would've won again.

I fought that chain for what seemed like forever. Sweat poured off me, and rust covered my hands and face and t-shirt. Finally, the chain felt wet with water from the well. My eyes were shut tight with determination as I kept trying to lift the bucket the last few feet to free it from the well-pipe. At last, the bucket appeared, dripping water from its sides. It cleared the well-pipe. I had done it!

I looked up at Grandpa, victory on my face. And then came an unexpected surprise. All the time I had been fighting "the Battle of the Bucket," Grandpa had been towering above me. And now, as I looked up at him, I saw him holding the chain in his powerful right hand, just where it came across the pulley. Every time I'd reached for a new section of chain he'd been holding my "purchase." If he hadn't been holding on for me, the bucket would have fallen back down into the well every time I reached up for another grip, and I couldn't have managed it. But in that moment, that didn't matter to me. I had finally drawn the water out of the well.

We emptied the bucket into a pail, and Grandpa said, "Remember now, if'n you raise the water outta the well, you have t' carry it up the hill t' the house."

I had assumed that Grandpa would carry the big bucket up to the house. My mistake. This struggle was not only a matter of overcoming the bucket's weight, but of having the fortitude to see the whole task through to the end. It dawned on me that Grandma's "stick-to-it-ive-ness" was gonna be called for.

I started up the hill, trying to hold the thin wire handle of the heavy pail of water steady in both hands and walking awkwardly to keep the water from sloshing out. I hadn't gone ten steps before the wire made deep red marks in my rust-covered palms, so I swallowed my pride, and asked, "Grandpa, can I borrow your gloves?"

"Sure," Grandpa said, and gave them to me.

Even then, I knew Grandpa was teaching me some kind of life lesson. His silence made that clear enough. But I couldn't think what it might be.

As we neared the house, I asked, "Grandpa, did I pull the water up or not?" I was beginning to have my doubts, but I was trying to be honest about them and sniff out Grandpa's lesson.

"Yep, you pulled it up, alright."

"But did I really pull it up all by myself?" I didn't know if it counted.

"Nobody ever pulls the water up all by 'umselves," he said.

That was another surprise. I'd seen Grandpa draw the water many times, and he did it all by himself. "You do, Grandpa," I said.

He didn't say anything.

We climbed the steps to the back porch. Grandma had the screen door into the kitchen open for us. As we entered, Grandpa announced, "Billy just pulled up his first bucket of water outta the well."

Grandma caught my eye. "Did, did he?" she said. "Well, in that case, I guess he'd be ready t' go out back and bring in the wood so's we can get breakfast goin.'"

I was exhausted, and my hands burned as if I had lowered the bucket all the way down into an elfin fireplace instead of a well, and pulled a red-hot bucket of coals seventy feet to the surface. I'd been expecting some praise from Grandma. But like Grandpa, she offered no praise, no trophy. She just figured that I was growing up, and therefore, able to do more to help around the farm.

Later, Grandpa said that I shouldn't expect to get any praise for doing what was expected. He called that "humility." But I'd succeeded drawing my first bucket of water from the well, and thought I deserved some recognition for my victory. I felt proud of myself, and it didn't make any sense to me that I shouldn't.

The next morning, we went down to the well again. Grandma needed fresh water in the kitchen.

"Grandpa," I said, "did I pull the water up out of the well yesterday, or not?" I was still stuck on that point.

"You did, and you didn't," he said.

"What's that supposed to mean?"

"Billy, you pulled the water outta the well all by yerself—but you didn't pull the water outta the ground all by yerself."

Now he'd confused me. I hadn't been expecting that. "What's the difference, Grandpa?"

"There'd be a big difference. You see, there were other folks who were there helpin' you, even though you didn't see 'um—just like they helped me. The well-digger—that'd be me—helped you get the water outta the ground. The man who built the special bucket t' draw the water helped you. The one who's kept the aquifer flowin' free and clear fer all these years helped you. Grandma, who's been feedin' you chicken 'n' dumplins' all these years t' help you build up yer strength; she was there helpin' you. All these people helped you. You couldn't have drawn the water outta the ground without 'um, so don't go off feelin' all proud-like, believin' that you did it all by yerself. It'd be a good lesson fer you. Nobody ever does a big job by himself, and that'd be includin' me."

After that, I felt a little better about the help Grandpa had given me. It was another lesson in humility, but I figured that if Grandpa could admit that it took more than his own strength to draw the water from the well, I could too.

The next morning, we went down to the well again to draw the water, and Grandpa helped me. Together, we pulled the water bucket up until it cleared the well-pipe. As we filled the pail with fresh water, I said, "Everyone needs help, don't they, Grandpa?"

"Yep," he said. "Everyone needs help."

And that was when I knew. More than drawing the water out of the well by myself, this lesson was what Grandpa had wanted me to learn all along. Somehow, Grandpa had been planning this, ever since I was nine years old. He was always doing that with every new encounter I had on the farm, the stoic Puritan teaching his grandson by way of hard experience. It was like boot camp—no explanations provided, no excuses allowed. He rarely said, "Billy, here's the lesson," or added any explanation to the moment. He wanted me to figure it out for myself. But he never left me confused. He guided my thinking until I finally got the point. And that was alright because everyone needs a helping hand from time to time.

Grandpa taught me that when I needed help, there was no shame in asking for someone else to hold my "purchase." That didn't mean I hadn't done the job myself. It just meant that everyone needs help.

As I grew older, Grandpa expected more and more help from me. Each new task challenged my humility. But the wrestling matches of this world are too heavy for anyone to manage alone, and the weight of heavy tasks was made lighter every time I dropped my pride, and humbly asked for help.

Now, It's Your Turn:

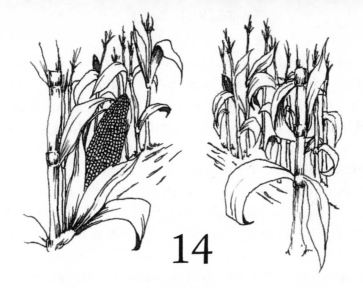

14

Grandpa Traps the Groundhog

Wisdom from the Farm:

You're the last person on this here Earth you're ever gonna be introduced t', so while you're tryin' t' figure out who you really are, take some counsel from the folks who love you the most. They can introduce you t' yerself 'cause they know you even better'n you know yerself.

Not much got under Grandpa's skin, so when something did, I remembered it. When the tobacco worm invaded his tobacco crop, that worked him up. Finding a red fox in Grandma's henhouse made him mad. If a pack of wild dogs on the loose took down one of his sheep in the night, he'd be out of sorts. One time, he discovered that the city fathers had wrongly taxed a man who had once worked for him, and he gave them no peace until they made it right. But nothing ever got Grandpa's goat like the groundhog.

It was an early August morning in 1957, the summer of my thirteenth year, when Grandpa discovered that overnight a groundhog had gotten into Grandma's vegetable garden. I found him rocking slowly in his cane bottom chair on the front porch, clinching a toothpick hard between his teeth. He was lost in a faraway stare. He was already thinking about how he was going to rid himself of this menace. In Grandpa's mind, a groundhog was a mortal enemy, and the unprovoked attack on Grandma's garden was a declaration of war.

About a month before, early in July, Grandpa had hired a bulldozer to move some dirt up against a low hill about five hundred yards south of the farmhouse. He was going to make a lake and stock it with fish to sell in town. The lake wasn't going to amount to much more than a pond—in fact, at sixty feet across, it was barely a puddle.

Soon after the lake was finished, a groundhog moved in. He tunneled into the soft earth that the bulldozer had pushed up to make the front lip of the lake and made a comfortable home for himself. From his front door looking across to the farmhouse, he had a great view of Grandma's big vegetable garden. It was real tempting, and being a groundhog, he felt that any vegetables that rose up out of the earth were fair game and had been put there for his benefit. The garden must have looked like a cafeteria to him, and he was the only one in line.

As soon as Grandpa discovered the unwelcome visitor, he began to make a plan to evict him. Two toothpicks into plotting his strategy—both of them chewed to splinters—Grandpa began to share the plan with me. I had finally reached my teens, and I guess he felt that I was old enough that he could confide in me.

First, he took me out to survey the battlefield.

"Grandpa, how come the groundhog made so many holes in the ground?" I said. There were over a dozen of them laid out randomly across the front embankment of the new lake. Either he had a big family, or he had some reason for needing a lot of back doors.

Grandpa explained, "That groundhog be diggin' a whole series of underground tunnels into the side of our lake, so's he'll always have an escape route. If'n one of the entrances caves in, or the groundhog's in danger, he'll escape right outta one of those exit tunnels."

"Does he have a family in there with him?" I asked.

"Nope. There'd be just one of him."

A few days later, Grandma's prized yellow squash suffered a devastating attack. Yellow squash grows right on top of the ground, so Grandma had taken extra measures to protect them from weeds and insects, and she had nursed them along, getting them ready to pick, cook, and put on the dinner table. She must have had thirty plants. Overnight, half the crop was destroyed. The remains lay half-eaten, broken off the vine, and already beginning to rot in the sun. It was a mess—a lot of backbreaking work gone to ruin.

Grandpa had had enough. He set about putting his plan into motion.

"What're you gonna do, Grandpa?" I said.

"Well, Billy," he said, as he chewed his third toothpick, "you're gonna help me."

"I am?"

"Yep!" he said. "Lemme tell you what we're gonna do."

"We're gonna siphon water outta the lake through a long hose. Then we're gonna stick the business end of the hose into one of the groundhog holes and try t' flood all his passageways at once."

"Okay," I said. "But what am I gonna do?" I was a little worried about that part.

He didn't answer me. Instead, he turned and set off toward the barn to retrieve the long hose that he kept coiled around an old tire rim up in the rafters.

The fact that Grandpa wouldn't tell me what he wanted me to do made me worry even more. But I figured that since he had nearly chewed clean through his fourth toothpick, an answer was coming soon.

I asked Grandma about what Grandpa was planning, but she didn't know.

"Billy," she said, "it's really a question of who's more clever—yer grandpa, or the groundhog." The image of the two of them pitted against one another must have really tickled her, because she started into one of her contagious laughing spells—but she caught herself up short, so that it wasn't much more than a long giggle. "With all this commotion over one groundhog..." She stopped again, because suddenly, the giggle looked like it might break out into a full-blown fit. Her eyes had gotten a humorous squint in them, and they were beginning to moisten up. But she held it in. She'd never let Grandpa see her laughing about something like this. He wouldn't have taken kindly to it.

Whenever Grandpa decided to draft me to help him do some unpleasant task on the farm, I never got any advance warning. I didn't know how I was going to be a part of Grandpa's plans until it was time to put them in motion. That didn't give me any time to prepare, and I needed some time to muster up my courage.

Since early July, when my family had first arrived on the farm, Grandpa and Dad had been teaching me to shoot the Remington single-shot .22 rifle. They figured thirteen should be old enough to begin learning to handle a firearm, and their opinion prevailed over Mom's objections.

Dad would pick up an Osage Orange—which was actually green, and looked like a big apple with a knobbly skin—and put it on top of one of the posts that held up the wire fencing that surrounded the garden to keep the cows and goats out. Then they'd back me up near one of the big cedar trees in the front yard, about fifty yards from the target, and load a .22-gauge cartridge into the rifle chamber. It was a single-shot rifle, so you only got one shot, and you'd better make it good.

I was never very good at it, even after practicing for weeks, but I liked it. It was fun, except on those occasions when my aim was on the mark, and that big green crinkly apple exploded into a mist with such violence that it disturbed something deep in my soul.

At that point, the inner part of my being still retained a bit of its original innocence. I had no idea what all this was leading up to.

On "Groundhog Day," Grandpa, with his fifth toothpick held firmly between his teeth, took me around behind the farmhouse. He had the rifle in one hand and a length of hose in the other. We hid behind the farmhouse so the groundhog couldn't see us coming. Seriously! Grandpa had never underestimated a groundhog, not once in all his life.

We left the shelter of the farmhouse and quietly circled the pond, so as to come at the groundhog's lodging from the side. Grandpa felt that a frontal attack might give away our strategy. The afternoon sunlight perfectly lit the side of the dirt wall that formed the front of the lake bed. Grandpa put one .22-gauge cartridge in my hand, gave the rifle to me, and then climbed up the hillside and put one end of the hose in the lake.

When he came back down, he said, "Billy, take the rifle, but don't chamber that round 'til we're directly in front of that sloppin' earthen wall." He pointed to show me exactly where we'd be standing, and whispered, "I'm gonna siphon water outta the lake and flood one of the tunnels, and I 'spect he'll have t' surface outta one of those two holes."

He pointed again, to be sure I saw which two he meant. Talking in a hushed, husky voice, he said, "Now, when you see a wet groundhog face surface outta one of those holes, I want you t' put a bullet right between his eyes. Be sure you hit him good, 'cause I'm gonna reach my hand down the hole and pull him outta there. If'n he's not dead, he's gonna bite off a finger at least."

My heart started beating fast. "Grandpa, wait. I can't do it," I said.

"Yeah, you can. You can do it," he said, and put his forefinger up to his lips as a sign that we had to be quiet. The discussion was over. He turned to walk up the bank and stick the hose in the lake.

My stomach tightened. I didn't have much confidence in my ability to hit what I aimed at. I really didn't want to do this thing, but if I didn't, Grandpa would be real disappointed in me. I was scared just short of tears, and I suddenly needed to pee real bad. Before I knew it, Grandpa was back at my side, with the hose just trickling a bit of water into his hand. He spat another toothpick out of his mouth and sucked hard on one end of the hose, and water began to pour out. Then he stuck the hose into one of the holes in the dirt, and the passageways began to fill.

It took longer to fill the network of tunnels than I expected, and my urge to pee was becoming stronger every minute. I could see the whole thing playing itself out before my eyes. The urge would soon overtake my ability to hold it back, and then I would be distracted; I would fire and miss hitting the critter between the eyes, and Grandpa would stick his hand into the water and the groundhog would bite off his finger. This was one of those defining moments in a young man's life.

At that very moment, the wet muzzle of the groundhog surfaced. I quickly aimed and fired.

The groundhog disappeared back under the water, and I couldn't tell whether I'd hit him or not. Grandpa didn't hesitate for a moment. He seemed more than willing to lose a finger at his grandson's expense. His whole arm went down into the water-filled hole. Either the groundhog was pulling him in, or he was trying to pull it out; I couldn't tell. I was shaking all over.

Then Grandpa reared back and pulled the groundhog out by the scruff of the neck, like you'd carry a small dog. The groundhog was dead, and Grandpa held him up with a big grin on his face and spit out his last toothpick. The battle was won.

I held the rifle by my side, every muscle shaking from the trauma of what I had done. I was so relieved and at the same time I felt hollow inside for the life I had taken.

"Grandpa, I was afraid I missed him."

"Nope. I knew you'd get him."

"But what if I had missed?"

"You didn't."

I could tell that he was real proud of me, but I couldn't stay to take it all in. I set the rifle down carefully, walked up the hill, and with great relief, peed into the lake, just at the moment of one of my greatest victories. It was real embarrassing.

Afterward, the realization that I had killed a living thing began to set in. It was such an empty sort of hurt. I felt like I was in shock, however being in shock felt, and my chest ached.

I wished I could say that I felt more alive than I ever had before, and hold my trophy high in the air and pose for a photograph, but it wasn't like that for me. Maybe I was a wuss. I wasn't sure.

But Grandpa thought I was good as churned butter. He clapped me on the shoulder with a bigger smile on his face than I ever remember seeing, and I was willing to play the part no matter how I felt inside. Maybe that was the lesson.

It felt like there were two ways of looking at me. On the inside, I wondered if I was a wuss. But on the outside, Grandpa thought I was apple pie. I couldn't figure out which trumped which. It seemed like "who I thought I was" should be more real than "who others thought I was." But I found out later, the "who" that the folks who really, truly love you think you are is usually closer to the truth than the "who" you think you are.

Grandpa once told me to "be slow t' judge yerself, 'cause you're the last person on this here Earth you're ever gonna be introduced t.'" So, that was it. I went with Grandpa. At least in his estimation, I was a good grandson. And Grandpa was the one person I wanted to be proud of me.

One thing's for sure: I've been hesitant to lift a rifle to my shoulder and shoot one of God's critters ever since. Even if I found a dinosaur in the cornfield, I don't think I would be able to pull the trigger. I'd just run. But then, I'm not a farmer.

Now, It's Your Turn:

_____

_____

_____

_____

_____

_____

_____

_____

_____

_____

_____

_____

_____

_____

_____

_____

_____

_____

_____

_____

_____

_____

15

Grandpa and the Only Clock That Counts

Wisdom from the Farm:

Life be like time—it'd be always movin' forward. But if'n somethin' or someone you love dies, it can stop you dead in yer tracks. It'd be a healthy thing t' stop and grieve fer a while, but stayin' stopped never resolves anythin'. You have t' get up and move on, carryin' yer regret, grief, and sorrow with you. Only when you be movin' forward is there hope of gettin' beyond the things in life that sometimes overwhelm yer desire t' live.

It was the summer of 1958. I was fourteen years old, and had formed opinions about a great many adult issues. I would gladly share these opinions with anyone who would listen—and that morning, the subject was milk.

Grandma and I were in the kitchen after breakfast, putting the breakfast fixings away in the refrigerator. Grandpa was waiting for me down by the barn; however Grandma and I were locked in a discussion about the merits of raw milk and store-bought milk. In the city, I was used to store-bought, but in the country, we drank milk straight from the cow. The milk we got from the dairy cows didn't taste like, smell like, or look like city-bought milk, and I didn't like it as much.

"Grandma," I said, "Raw milk straight from the cow, like the kind in the jug you just put in the fridge, just tastes different. It tastes a little weird. It's not as creamy as the milk we get in the city, and it smells…" I couldn't think of a word to describe the smell, "…bovine?"

"You'll get used t' it, and you'll be healthier fer it," Grandma said. "Wha' d'you mean when you say it smells bovine?"

"Well, I guess I mean that it smells like a cow, because I just milked the cow that gave that milk. Maybe it doesn't really smell different, but I can't help smelling 'cow' in my imagination. I associate the cow giving the milk with the final product. I just can't help it! It smells like 'cow' to me."

I was getting antsy. Now that I was fourteen, I was expected to do a lot more to help out around the farm. That morning I was supposed to meet Grandpa down at the barn right after breakfast and help him prepare the raw milk we had gotten from the Guernseys for pickup by the milk truck from the Borden's Dairy Company in Columbia. Grandma knew that. In fact, that was what had gotten us on the subject of milk in the first place.

The dairy truck arrived every morning before 9:00 a.m., and my talk with Grandma was making me late. I needed to bring the conversation to an end. But Grandma had staked out her position in this little discussion, and she wasn't finished.

"Billy, I know you're used t' drinkin' citified milk, but the milk you're used t' isn't as good fer you as raw milk. It's been pasteurized. The pasteurization process makes that milk sterile. All the good enzymes and minerals have been removed."

I'd studied how milk was processed in school, but I couldn't remember what pasteurization did to the milk. If by "sterile," she meant "sanitized," then she'd made my point for me: milk from the store was cleaner than milk straight from the cow.

Taking a couple steps away from Grandma and toward the kitchen door, I said, "Grandma, I'm in a hurry to help Grandpa prepare the milk to be picked up. Besides," I added, "I just like the milk in the city better. It's cleaner, and it gets colder, and it doesn't have that layer of fatty cream on top every time you take it out of the fridge."

"Cleaner!" she said. "It can't be any cleaner than when it comes straight from nature!"

I held my hand up, as if I were pushing back from her argument. "I've got to catch up to Grandpa. He's expecting me. Can we talk about this again later?"

Before she could respond, I turned and ran through the house, out the front door, and started down the hill toward the barn. Over the years, I had finally learned how to hurry down that hill without tripping and falling on the loose pebbles.

I spotted Grandpa down by the barn, pouring the contents of one of that morning's milk pails into a large ten-gallon commercial milk can.

"Grandpa, I'm coming!" I hollered. In the back of my mind, I was afraid I'd be too late. I didn't want to miss the excitement of the pickup, when the truck gathered milk cans from our farm to be taken to the processing plant, where the milk would be pasteurized and become the kind of milk I liked.

"Are we too late to catch the truck, Grandpa?" I said breathlessly as I reached him. "What time is it?"

As soon as I asked, I remembered that Grandpa didn't wear a wristwatch. On prior occasions when I'd asked him for specific information like, "Grandpa, how much longer until noon?" he would pull out a broken pocket watch he kept in the pocket of his overalls, glance at it, and then give me his best guess. Usually,

Grandpa's best guess was good enough for me. It was only now that I realized Grandpa had no way of telling time.

Grandpa wasn't about to ignore my question. He looked around to see how the sun cast its light on the farmland, judging its angle and intensity. Then he said, "I reckon it'd be 'bout eight o'clock. The truck won't be along fer a while yet."

He wasn't off by much. We had just gotten the milk cans in place on the wooden shelf outside the fence beside the roadway, when the Borden's Milk truck arrived. It braked hard, crunching gravel under its tires, and two men jumped out.

Grandpa tipped his hat to them. "Mornin', Frank. Mornin', Lefty."

They returned his greeting briefly, in a hurry because of all the stops they had to make. They had the "pickup" down to a fine routine. As the truck came to a stop, they jumped out and got up on the back tailgate of the truck as one of them, groaning under the weight, hefted a heavy milk can and passed it to the other. With shouts, and a clanging of metal, they fit our milk cans in among a lot of others of different sizes. Then they leaped down from the truck, slammed the tailgate, ran around to the front doors, and jumped inside. With arms extended out the windows, a cordial wave, and a spray of crushed rock from the roadway as the tires fought for traction, they were off to the next pickup. All of it took two minutes or less. They checked their watches to see if they were "on time." That would be Borden Milk Truck time.

Grandpa and I watched them disappear into the dust as they sped up, traveling down the road toward the church. After they were out of sight, Grandpa and I opened the gate, and started up the hill to the house, carrying a couple of glass jugs full of milk for the family to enjoy—raw milk, straight from Mother Nature.

On the way, I asked Grandpa if I could see his pocket watch. He fished it out of his pocket and showed it to me. The hands were set to 4:30.

"Grandpa, did you set your watch this morning?"

"No use," he said. "This watch be broken. I go by farm time."

"Why do you carry that pocket watch if it's broken?"

"'Cause this watch prompts me t' check nature's clock, by readin' the signs on the farm—like the angle that the light's strikin' the trees. Then I reset the time on the watch. Later, if'n I go t' wonderin' what time it is, I pull out the watch t' see what time it was the last time I set it. Judgin' by how much time I thinks passed, I can make a good guess as t' what time it must be now."

"Grandpa, you need to buy a new watch."

"Nope," he said. "There'd be no need. Farm time be good enough for me. On sunny days, the farm'd be one big sundial— the angle of the sunlight makin' shadows on the ground tells me what time it is. On a cloudy day, the animals tell me when it'd be time t' be fed, the dairy cows remind me when it'd be time t' be milked, and Grandma rings the farm bell at mealtime. If'n you keep track of all these things, you'll have a good idea what time it is."

"But, Grandpa, if you had a watch that worked, then you'd always know exactly what time it is."

"May be, but on a farm, you don't need t' know exactly what time it is. Knowin' exactly what time it is only creates worry in you. Farm time be measured in mealtimes, the day of the week, and the season of the year, and if'n you keep track of the days and seasons of nature, you'll always be on time, far as the farm's concerned. A farm's got a clock of its own."

"What kinda clock has the farm got, Grandpa?"

"Wha' d'you mean, what kinda clock? A clock's a clock," he said. "It's a clock that tells you what time it is."

I decided to spoof him. "Grandpa, if the farm's got a clock, how come I never hear it go off?"

"Maybe 'cause you're not listenin' t' the earth," he said.

"But you can hear it, right, Grandpa?"

"Yep," he said. He didn't realize I was spoofing him—or if he did, he didn't let on. We walked the rest of the way in silence.

That was the day I became interested in Grandpa's concept of time. I began to realize that while the exact time of day was important in the city, on the farm, the more important measures of time were not so much the minute and the hour, but the day and the season. That was why Grandpa didn't need a watch. Instead, Grandpa measured time by combining his understanding of the farm clock with his own personal bio-logical clock. For example: He knew that if it had been real late in the morning, say 11:00 a.m., Grandma would have rung the farm bell announcing the midday meal. His own stomach would tell him that it wasn't anywhere near lunchtime—but he knew that it had been a while since breakfast at 7:00 a.m. So, according to his bio-logical clock, it must be around 9:00 a.m. That same clock got him up in the morning and put him to sleep each night.

Grandpa's bio-logical clock extended to weekly measurements, too. On the farm, there were no calendars on the walls of the house to keep one day separate from another— though it helped that every Saturday was Market Day in town. Market Day served as another "marker day" during the week. Grandpa went to town every Saturday, and on Sunday, he reset his internal clock to the day of the week. How many work days had it been since Sunday? Two days? Well, then, it was Tuesday. How many working days 'til next Sunday? Three days? Then it must be Thursday.

But as important as it was to tell the hour by the angle of the sun, the moisture in the air, or how hungry your stomach was starting to feel since breakfast; or the day by how many days it had been since Sunday, it was more important for a farmer like Grandpa to be able to tell time by the "seasons of the soil." If a farmer didn't know the "seasons of the soil," he might miss the ideal planting time by a couple of weeks, and when it came time to harvest the crop, it wouldn't have produced any good vegetables.

Many farmers used the *Farmer's Almanac* to tell them what day to plow and when to sow and when to harvest—but not Grandpa. Grandpa could tell what season it was in the soil by the length of the day, the moisture on the ground in the early morning, and the day a particular tree or flower began to bud.

Sometimes when I asked Grandpa what time it was, he would answer with the time it was according to his "seasons of the soil" clock. On those occasions, our conversations usually went something like this:

"Grandpa, what time is it?" I would say. And he would answer:

"It'd be late March. But the soil's too damp. If'n Grandma plants her early peas now, the seed's liable t' rot in the ground, and she wouldn't get her peas. But if'n it doesn't rain over the weekend, and the soil's dried out some by next week, when the mornin' sun'll be a little more direct, then it'll be 'bout the right time fer Grandma t' plant her early seed."

Or: "It'd be late April, and the tulip poplar just started bloomin', so it'd be time t' shear the sheep."

Or: "It'd be late August, and the yellow cookin' apples are beginnin' t' fall from the branch, so it'd be time t' pick 'um."

Or: "It'd be mid-November, and the soil has dried out, and we haven't had a frost yet, so it'd be 'bout time t' plow under the stubble left over from the harvest."

Or: "It'd be December, and we had our first frost last night. So I reckon it'd be 'bout time t' butcher the hog."

But there was yet another clock to which Grandpa and the farming community calibrated themselves. It used a measure of time to which people in the big city didn't seem to pay much attention. That clock was the most important of all, and it was called the "seasons of life" clock.

Once, when I was twelve, I had asked Grandpa to explain the "seasons of life" clock to me.

"It tells you what time it'd be in yer life," he told me.

"You mean like how old I am?"

"Nope! This clock doesn't measure how old you are. It'd be tellin' the time like the Good Book explains when it says, 'There's a time t' weep and a time t' laugh,' 'There's a time t' mourn and a time t' dance,' 'There's a time t' build up and a time t' tear down that which was built,' and 'There's a time t' be silent and a time t' speak.' You get the idea?"

"Yeah, I think so," I said. "If it's a season in your life for weeping, then you're meant t' cry and not hide your hurt, and if it's a season in your life for laughing, then you're meant to laugh."

"That'd be 'bout right. Like the Bible says, the "seasons of life" clock helps us t' recognize what season it is in our lives, and then enter into that season fully. Grievin' in a "season of mournin'" be just as healthy fer yer body and spirit as laughin' be in a time fer happiness."

I wasn't aware of it at the time, but when I was almost fifteen, the "seasons of life" clock shifted for me. That was the year I stopped making regular visits to see Grandma and Grandpa on the farm. It was time to get on with my education—first in high school, and then in college. Working summer jobs to help pay my way left me with no opportunity to make my summer visits to the farm. After that, it was time for me to start a career, then it was time to marry and start a family. After that, it was time to begin fulfilling my "calling" as a minister. Almost before I knew it, the season of life that I had known and loved, when the family visited Grandpa and Grandma in the winters and summers, had passed.

As I moved past the season for childhood visits to the farm, I knew I should mourn the passing of that time—but I also realized that this new time was a time for building, so I needed to give myself fully to building. That was how the "seasons of life" clock worked. Sometimes important things, like visiting the farm, had to be left behind—until something happened that brought me back to the farm one more time.

I was twenty-nine years old when Grandma died, and for a while, my world stopped. The family traveled back to Rock Spring together one more time, to make arrangements and take care of Grandpa. According to the calendar, it was July of 1973— but for us, it was a "season of life" time, a time to participate in the "dying" time of life.

Grandma's funeral service was held in Columbia, at the Oakes and Nichols Funeral Home. We buried her in the old Rock Springs Cemetery, which sat up on a hill across from the Rock Springs Church on the other side of Sowell Mill Pike. By the time everyone had driven out into the country and arrived at the cemetery, it was nearly 1:00 p.m., and being July, the heat was rising. The long black hearse was already there, and the pallbearers had taken Grandma's casket out to the gravesite. We started to get out of the car to go stand around the grave where the preacher would read the Word and bow his head to pray.

But Grandpa didn't get out of the car. He sat in the front seat with the window rolled down, and said that he could hear the preacher just fine from there.

As I got out of the backseat, I took a quick look at Grandpa, who was staring across the hilltop toward the people gathering around, and I saw one tear roll down his stubbled cheek. I didn't say anything to him. I didn't know what to say. There was no change in his expression. Just that one tear, slowly trickling down his weathered cheek. What time was it? Didn't matter. It was a "season of life" time called "dying."

After the service, we all got back in the car and went to Aunt Nina's for a meal. Everyone was standing around and talking. Grandpa sat by himself in a wicker chair leaning back against the wall, and didn't say much, except to thank a friend for coming.

Then it was over. Grandpa picked up and went on with his life. It would never be the same—but what time was it? It was "time to get up and move on with life." You didn't need a watch to know that.

That was a hard day for me. Mostly, I felt empty inside, and real sad for Grandpa. I wasn't sure how he felt, but I felt like I had lost someone who was very important in my life, and I knew I would never be able to go back and relive those days with her. I regretted that my last talk with Grandma had been about something as mundane as milk. I wished instead that I'd told her I loved her. It hurt me to think that that morning when I was fourteen, I hadn't checked the time on the "Clock that Counts." It would have been so easy to just say, "Grandma, I love you," before I ran down to the barn to be with Grandpa. For me, the grieving was a real physical hurt in the chest—one of those inner sorrows of the heart that really ached. I felt lost, and didn't know where to go from there.

I wished I could talk to Grandpa about it, but I thought he might be feeling the same, so I didn't. For a while, it felt like time had stopped. But in a couple of days, to my surprise, it seemed as if someone started the clock again, and things began to happen more like they should. The cows needed to be milked, and the Borden Milk Truck stopped by at the usual time. Someone had to come and do the things that Grandma used to take care of, like hoeing in the garden and preparing meals. The routine on the farm started up again as if nothing important had changed.

Two days after Grandma's funeral, early in the morning, Grandpa went up to the cemetery by himself for a couple of hours. There was one lonely tree in the cemetery, but it was a big tree. Being a spreading elm, it was true to its name. Its limbs stretched way out, so that the shade it provided covered most of the gravestones.

There was always a cool breeze on that hilltop, even in the hottest part of the summer. I found it strange for there to always be a breeze, in what was in all other ways, a dying-place—but somehow, I liked standing on that hill and feeling that breeze. It seemed to whisper saying, "Now, don't you worry none. It may look t' you like life's gone stone-cold dead here on this lonely hilltop, but I'm sending this fresh breeze blowin' through the elm tree t' remind you that the people you love are still alive. Sometimes you can feel their presence like you feel this breeze, even if you can't see them."

As I sat on the front porch step, waiting for Grandpa to come home from the cemetery, I said a quiet prayer. I hoped that he felt the comforting breeze, and heard it speak to him.

When I saw him start up the hill toward the house, I stood to greet him—but I didn't know what to say. He motioned for me to sit in one of the wicker chairs on the farmhouse porch amid Grandma's morning glories—which strangely went on blooming without her—and sat beside me. I had a feeling a story might be coming—and sure enough, I was right.

"Billy," he began, "way back when the pioneers were first comin' through this way, 'round about 1800 or so, there'd be this family headin' west fer the Missouri Territory. They passed through our farm in their wagon, and when they crossed the old Sowell Mill Pike, they made camp fer the night by the stream that flowed past the base of Elm Tree Hill. They camped right below the hill, where the cemetery is now. Their young daughter was lyin' in the wagon, real sick with the fever. And that night, the little girl died."

He went on, "The hill with the elm tree on top belonged t' the Jones family, and when the child passed that evening, the pioneer father climbed the hill t' the Jones' farmhouse and asked if he could bury his little daughter under the elm tree on the crest of the hill, directly above where the family had made their camp. Brother Jones and his wife, Matty, went down and comforted the family, and the next morning they buried the child under the spreadin' elm. After the burial, the family broke camp and continued their journey on t' the Missouri Territory. Their little girl was the first t' be buried in Rock Spring Cemetery."

He continued, "That family didn't bury their daughter lightly. I 'spect they grieved her loss fer months. But death be a season of life—and all seasons pass, and life goes on. As badly as that family hurt, they believed that in time, their season of grief would give way t' a season of new life."

I understood what Grandpa was trying to tell me: you didn't need a watch to tell you how long you ought to stop and grieve, but you couldn't just sit there and let yourself waste away when there was land waiting for you to come and tend to it. So when the sun came up, you hitched the horses to the wagon, and you went on, carrying your grief with you. You moved forward, and somehow, the act of moving forward gradually helped you heal.

Grandpa went on. "Movin' on is an exercise in faith. No doubt that pioneer family knew the scripture from the Old Bible that said, 'To everythin'—includin' grief and sorrow—there is a season.'"

This was starting to sound a little familiar. I was an ordained minister by then and knew the passage Grandpa was referring to. But around Grandpa, I was still the student learning from the teacher. "What scripture is that, Grandpa?"

"It'd be in the Old Bible, the Book of Ecclesiastes, Chapter Three." Grandpa knew his Bible. "Billy, there'd be a preacher-man once, a long, long time ago—I reckon it was thousands of years ago—who preached a right good sermon 'bout time. Someone who was there must'a thought it was real important, 'cause they wrote it down. In the sermon, the preacher describes God's clock, and says that that's the only clock that counts."

I didn't know whether Grandpa was finished with his thought or not, but I had an important question I needed to ask. "Grandpa, what will happen to the farm when you aren't here to take care of it? Will it keep blooming, like Grandma's morning glories?"

Grandpa was real quiet for a long time. Maybe he was wrestling with the question of letting go. Letting go of a season you loved in a place you loved with people you loved and moving on, can be a hard thing to do.

Grandpa finally broke the silence. He looked out on the farm, where we had shared so many adventures. "Oh, the farm will be fine. It'll rest fer a while, and then we'll sell it t' someone who will take care of it the way we took care of it. We owned the farm fer a while, but it never belonged t' us. We took care of it fer a while, and it took care of us, but the time's come fer us t' let it go. Lettin' go. That'd be our new season of life."

"Can you do that, Billy? Can you be thankful fer what the farm meant, and at the same time, be lettin' it go?"

The question caught me by surprise. "I don't know, Grandpa. I think I'll always remember it the way it is now. But I won't know what's happening to it, and that may worry me some."

"Me, too," he said. "But I have t' trust that the farm'll be in hands bigger and better'n my own. If'n I can trust that that's true, then I'll be able t' let it go."

He was quiet again for a moment, and then he said, "It'd be the same with Grandma. We never owned her, and now we have t' trust that she's in the arms of her Maker. We could never love her as much as He can. If'n we can trust the Maker t' take care of her, then we'll be able, in time, t' let her go. We'll keep her memory with us, but we'll let her go.

"Billy, the end of that sermon is special."

"How does it end, Grandpa?"

"The preacher finished up by sayin', 'And God set eternity into the heart of man, so's he couldn't tell what God was doin' from the beginnin' t' the end.'"

"The end?" I said.

"I reckon he meant the end of time."

"Tell me more, Grandpa."

"Well, the preacher allowed we could remember the best of the past and think 'bout the future as bein' good, but we won't be able t' understand all the "why" questions that come t' us from time t' time. We just have t' trust God, and if'n we can trust God t' take care of all those things, then we can move from one season of life t' the next and not be 'fraid."

"Go on, Grandpa."

"I reckon it means that the Maker gave His children the power t' imagine eternity. That way, they would always know there will be a future full of happiness in a better world—but He didn't give 'um the knowledge t' understand all the 'why' and the 'how' and the 'when' questions. Fer those questions, you just have t' trust.

"The preacher-man was tryin' t' say, 'Don't be worryin' 'bout what time it'd be, 'cause God knows what time it is; and He allows you t' rest yer mind on the meanin' of time, but not worry 'bout it. Just live every day fully. And even if'n someone you love dies, that person's still alive somewhere else, but you won't be able t' fully understand it, and there will be questions that come t' you, but you won't be able t' answer 'um.'"

Grandpa explained that it didn't matter what time it was, because God has control of every day, and God will take care of all the truly important things for us. Perhaps what Grandpa was trying to say was that it was okay to wear a watch, so long as I didn't worry too much about what time it was, because God has the only clock that counts.

"I understand, Grandpa," I said. Secretly, I wanted to know that while he was grieving Grandma, he could still move on with his life. Tomorrow would be the third day after the funeral, and most of the family would be leaving. But Grandpa had to stay, and live out a new "season of life."

The next day, the family left to go back home and get on with our lives. Dad stayed behind to help Grandpa get moved into a nursing home in Columbia. Grandpa was getting frail, and there was no one left to take care of him on the farm.

That would be my last visit to the place where I had learned so much about growing up. Without Grandpa there, going back really wouldn't feel the same. But Grandpa was right when he said that God's watch is the only one that really works—it runs on for eternity. Although many years have since passed, in my heart the farm feels as much alive to me now as it ever did.

Now, It's Your Turn:

_____

_____

_____

_____

_____

_____

_____

_____

_____

_____

_____

_____

_____

_____

_____

_____

_____

_____

_____

_____

_____

_____

16

The Miracle of the Last Silver Dollar

Wisdom from the Farm:

There'd be times when you lose somethin' and never miss it. You live yer life and never realize that there's somethin' of great value you be doin' without. Then, all unexpected, someone gives you back what you've been livin' without, and when you get it back, you realize what a treasure you'd been missin'. You'll live a happier life if'n you live yer life believin' that one day, yer treasure will come back t' you.

A
t the end of each summer, before our family left the farm to head back to the city, Grandpa would give my brother and me a couple of silver dollars from his stash. Grandpa saved mint silver coins, putting them in socks, and hiding the socks under his mattress. At least that's where we figured he hid them. My brother and I never caught him at it, so we never knew for sure where the "mother lode" might be.

When Grandma had passed, and Grandpa was eighty-five, he left the farm and moved to the Graymere Nursing Home in

Columbia. From time to time, while visiting in-laws in Ohio, I would drive down to visit him. By this time, I was about thirty-eight years old, and at my age, some part of me thought Grandpa ought to have shifted from calling me "Billy" to calling me "Bill." But when he greeted me, I was still "Billy." To him, I was still the little boy on the farm.

I was sitting in Grandpa's room, reading to him from the articles he had clipped out of the *Daily Herald*. Most of them had to do with the building of the Columbia Dam on the Duck River. He was real interested in whether that dam would be built. A lot of political wrangling and lawyering was in motion, as people tried to stop the Tennessee Valley Authority from pursuing the project. If the measure did go through, a small part of Grandpa's farm might be flooded, returning the land to the watery depths from which it had emerged so many millions of years before.

One environmental group had discovered that a particular variety of mussel, the birdwing pearlymussel, made the Duck River its natural habitat. This mussel was unique to the Duck River basin and other small streams in Tennessee and Virginia. Some groups were lobbying to keep the Duck River free of further development in order to protect the mussel. If the project passed, the building of the dam could be the death knell for this endangered species. It would become extinct in one generation.

I wasn't sure whether Grandpa was for the completion of the dam or against it. Even at that age, he kept his own counsel.

The suits and countersuits went on for years. Eventually, the issue went all the way to the United States Supreme Court. Imagine—the highest court in the land, spending all that time debating over a tiny mussel living in the crookedest river in the world. But it gave Grandpa something to care about. Would the mussel win out, or would the TVA dam prevail?

On this particular occasion, Grandpa had something more important on his mind than mussels and the TVA dam. Of all my trips over the span of his ten-year stay in the nursing home, this particular visit in the fall of 1983 was to be the most memorable. I was about to experience the "silver dollar" tradition one last time.

Our visit only lasted a couple of hours. I read to him, and we talked about the farm and his life in the nursing home. Later, Grandpa allowed me to roll him in his wheelchair to the dining hall. After dinner I rolled him back, and we said our goodbyes. I needed to hit the road to get back to Cincinnati before midnight.

I didn't know it at the time, but that was the last time I would see my grandpa before his death. Had I known, I would have said many things. I would have told him how much my childhood on the farm had meant to me. Maybe I would have had the courage to tell him I loved him, but that was a subject that was understood between Hardison men, and seldom spoken.

I don't remember much of what I said. But I do remember our last exchange. Just as I was leaving, Grandpa stopped me and reached into the drawer of the lampstand next to his bed. He pulled out a sock he had hidden away, far in the back of the drawer. From the sock, he drew out a shiny silver dollar, and said that he wanted me to have it.

As he put it into my hand, he said, "Billy, d'you recognize this coin?"

I saw that it was an 1889 Morgan silver dollar. But I couldn't distinguish it from any other silver dollar he had pulled out of his sock over the years.

So I said, "No, Grandpa. I don't recognize it."

"I figured you might not. It's been a lotta years since you've seen it."

He said, "Billy, I want t' tell you the story of this silver dollar 'cause it's a part of yer growin'-up years on the farm." And he began to tell the story, right then and there.

"'Bout when you were just a little tyke, maybe six years old, I gave you this very same silver dollar. You put it in the shallow pocket of yer knickers, and while you and yer brother be runnin' 'cross the hillside there below the farmhouse where we found the fossil, this here coin jumped clean outta yer pocket and lay among the rocks on that hillside."

He went on: "One day, been 'bout five years ago, I was goin' through the old farmhouse. By then, it was all overgrown with vines." He told me how the cedar shake roof that had saved us in the monster storm had caved in over the old bedroom. The stone chimney that had been in the bedroom, providing the firelight by which I had often fallen asleep, was still intact, and the spot by the window where Grandma had read to us by the light of the old Aladdin oil lamp was still there; but the walls of the room, now exposed to the elements, were heavily weathered.

"Be on that day," he said, "I spotted a hole in the wall of the bedroom where the peelin' wallpaper had been pullin' back. When I stuck my hand into the hole, I pulled out a little treasure trove of things that a pack rat had been bankin' fer several years.

"Billy, did you know that a pack rat will swap objects that he loves fer almost anythin' shiny? He'd be very civilized 'bout such things. He never picks up someone's chewin' gum wrapper without leavin' somethin' shiny in its place.

"Among the treasures that this pack rat had saved up was this silver coin. It was the same one you lost that day, so many years ago. I remember the mint date was 1889. The pack rat had been scrummagin' 'round on that hillside among the rocks and found what you'd lost. He left some shiny foil and a thimble in its place, and removed this silver coin to his 'hole in the wall' vault.

"Now, I'm returnin' it t' you. You were too young t' handle it when you were six years old, but I believe that you're old enough now t' know its true worth."

I didn't know what to say. A part of my history had found its way back to me. Over thirty-two long years, that silver dollar had come full circle: from Grandpa to me to the rocky hillside to the pack rat and back to Grandpa; and now it was mine again. Somehow, it seemed fated that I was to receive this precious gift from my grandfather.

For the first time ever, I understood why every silver dollar he gave us was so shiny. He got them in mint condition from the bank, and preserved that mint condition by storing them away secretly. He never got them out to count them. He never spent them. He had one and only one purpose: he wanted to teach us how to keep them in mint condition. He wanted us to learn to put them away in our own hiding places and not spend them. He wanted us to learn to save them, so that one day, they would be of greater value to his grandchildren than they ever were to him.

I'd always thought Grandpa was poor. After all, just how much old, grey, lifeless prehistoric rock could this miracle-making mystic of the land turn into nourishing yellow grain? Even a miracle has its limitations.

When Grandpa died in 1984, at the age of ninety-four, we all celebrated a life well lived and began to cherish the life lessons he had taught us. But Grandpa had one last surprise in store for us—one we definitely had not expected.

For seventy years, Grandpa had been turning old grey rock into golden grain as if he were a medieval alchemist. Because thrift was one of his character traits (a trait that didn't seem to have passed on to me), he had turned the worthless rock into riches.

When my dad closed Grandpa's bank account in Columbia, we discovered that he had compiled a hefty sum of $90,000. That was back in 1984. The equivalent sum in 2017 would amount to nearly $200,000, adjusted for inflation.

By the time he died, Grandpa had four great-grandchildren. When my dad realized how much money Grandpa had put away, he decided to turn the whole amount into a college fund for his grandchildren—Lēgie's great-grandchildren. Dad felt that this was something that his father would have wanted. Knowing my grandpa as well as I did, I understood that he would have loved knowing that his life's work resulted in his four great-grandchildren having a chance to attend college.

So my dad wisely reinvested all of his inheritance, earmarking it for the education of Grandpa's great-grandchildren. He put it away like Grandpa had done before him. Over the next ten years, it accumulated interest, until one by one, the grandchildren became old enough to go to college. By then, it amounted to a whole lot of money—alchemized prehistoric rock brought back to life.

As it turned out, the Tennessee Valley Authority didn't build the dam. The mussel won. But in the 1990s, Toyota built a huge assembly plant in Columbia, and Monsanto moved its headquarters to town. Thousands of new workers arrived knowing nothing about the farm. New, modern communities sprang up to meet the housing needs of so many newcomers. The farm that had been so remote became a far suburb of the city, and the land that had been the farm was sold and parceled out to make room for single-family housing.

Many years later, Dad told me that, in the process of transforming the farm into suburbs, the developers didn't send in bulldozers to grade away the hills as he had feared. The lower fossil field still lies at the foot of the hill. The boulders are gone, and the field has been turned into a huge lawn. The old farmhouse has given way to a modern suburban home. The tree line where Grandpa and I set up traps and caught the old red fox remains unchanged. The upper forty, which we often plowed; and Cranford Hollow, where my great-great-grandfather was shot and killed, all look about the same. Of course, the Rock Spring Road has been improved dramatically, and the land on both sides parceled off into two-acre lots. Even the old pecan tree in the front yard is still standing with my initials showing where Grandpa had cut them into the bark. And perhaps some young boy not unlike myself, full of imagination, looks at those initials and imagines that an old pioneer in a wagon train carved them on his way to the western frontier with his family.

I am getting to be an old pioneer, but I'm taking my stories with me. They are part of who I am, and they help me find my way whenever I am lost. They are my legacy.

Maybe one day I'll go back, but it won't be the same. I do have wonderful memories, and a silver dollar that was a gift my grandfather gave to me—twice.

I kept that old silver dollar in my dresser drawer at home for the next forty years. One day, I took it out. I had forgotten before, but the mint date stamped on the shiny silver was 1889, just as Grandpa said. Grandpa had been born in 1889. Somehow, that made the coin even more special.

Still, I wondered how much the old coin was really worth. I hadn't kept it in mint condition. I took it to a coin collector, almost ashamed that I was even trying to learn its monetary worth. Its true worth was the memories that it held of a childhood spent on a broken-down old rock-strewn farm that to anyone else would seem like a "no-where," but to me had become a treasured "some-place." It is a place that, as I sit down with my memories, is still alive with meaning for me.

"How much?" I said, leaning across the counter as the collector examined its condition.

"Well," he said, "these Morgan silver dollars are real collectors' items. One of the most beautiful coins ever minted in the United States. Look here on the back," he said. "Do you see this little 'o'?"

"Yes, what does that mean?" I asked.

"It means that this silver dollar was stamped in the New Orleans mint. It was made from the last of the silver mined in Nevada in the early 1800s, before the mine gave out. I'd say it's worth around $120." I was stunned. A silver dollar worth $120!

He wasn't finished. "Now, if that little 'o' had been a 'cc,' it would be worth close to $9,000."

Wow, I thought, *that's incredible*. But it didn't matter anyway. Even if it had been worth $10,000, it held far more value than that to me. It was the symbol of the gift of wisdom my grandpa had taught me, and the special days we spent together so many years ago. Those days and the lessons I learned are more precious to me than anything else I own.

Now, It's Your Turn:

_____

_____

_____

_____

_____

_____

_____

_____

_____

_____

_____

_____

_____

_____

_____

_____

_____

_____

_____

_____

_____

17

My Last Talk with Grandpa

Wisdom from the Farm:

If'n you want t' be content with yer life, you need t' pour a heap of livin' into belongin' t' the place where you are, and set aside the desire t' be someplace you aren't. If'n you believe that the most excitin' things in life are buried right under yer own two feet, right where you are, then there'd be no place on this here Earth where you can go and be any happier'n you can be, bein' right where you are.

Grandpa died on August 28, 1984, at the age of ninety-four. I attended his funeral in Columbia. As I listened at the graveside up on the hill above the old rock spring, standing in the breeze beneath the spreading elm, the pastor told of the many wonderful conversations he had enjoyed with Grandpa.

The only emotion I remember from that day is anger. I suppose that it was selfish of me to feel that way, but I was angry that Grandpa had had long conversations with the pastor, but had confided so little in me. There was so much I wanted to know, and now I never would. I needed to talk to Grandpa about intimate things; how he felt about his life, about his faith, about what made him the man he was. I wanted to know how he managed his own fears. I wanted to know how he could be so comfortable inside his own skin. I wanted to know how that was possible.

I needed to know these things, because I was lost in all these ways, and I knew that Grandpa had the answers that I needed to hear in order to find myself. So I felt angry. I wanted to know how Grandpa lived his life as a young man, my age. I had always related to him as a child would to a grandfather. I felt left out of so much of the part of his life in which he shared his adult feelings with another adult. I wanted to know that part of who Grandpa had been.

Through the years, I had asked him so many childish questions. Things like, "Hey, Grandpa, why do some of the chickens hog all the corn?" And he'd just sit and smile, and ask me stuff like, "Wha' d'you think?" And I'd say, "I don't know, Grandpa. I try to pitch some corn out to the shy ones, but they're always holding back, and the bigger ones always beat them to it."

"Noticed that, did you?" he said.

"Yes, Grandpa. Why is that?"

I'd spent my whole childhood asking Grandpa questions like that. And now that he was gone, I realized that there was one question I had really needed to ask—one that was more important than all the others combined. But I had missed my chance.

At that time, I was thirty-nine years old, and I knew that Grandpa had been a pivotal person in my life, but I didn't understand why. I had been telling the "Grandpa Stories" to various audiences for years. But I didn't know what they meant until March 24, 1987—three years after his death.

Before I continue, you should know that I am a person with a scientific mindset, and what I am about to share is way beyond what I would call normal. Usually, I wouldn't have entertained the sort of thing that I am about to share. But at that time, I was feeling desperate, experiencing a great deal of restlessness. For my entire adult life, I had moved every three or four years. I was never satisfied, never content. And I was seriously questioning my career choice.

I have to confess that I had a long struggle with my professional calling. When I went to college, I prepared to teach mathematics, but then changed my major to German. Finally, I settled on physics. I then went to graduate school at UNC-Chapel Hill to get a master's degree in Russian history, of all things; then to seminary to prepare for the ministry. It's not hard to see how confused I was.

After a brief time in the pastoral ministry, I moved again. Leaving the ministry behind, I wound up in Florida, teaching biology in a high school. But after four years, teaching no longer seemed fulfilling to me, and I decided to return to the ministry. I moved back to Virginia and took a pastorate in a parish in the Northern Neck. It was a very isolated region, and I missed the city.

After three years in the country, I accepted a call to take up the pastorate in a very attractive area near a major university in Richmond, Virginia. My wife and I made the move—but after six years at that assignment, I had an emotional burnout. I was lost, heading off in all directions at once. I was discontented with where I was and what I was doing. I knew Grandpa would've had the answer to my problem, just like he always had.

One day, I received in the mail an announcement of an Ira Progoff Workshop that was to be held at Union Theological Seminary in Richmond. The brochure said that I would learn the Progoff Journaling method, a process that provides a way for your conscious self to slow down and reflect deeply. In this system, your subconscious self sometimes does your journaling for you. It seemed to border on the magical. But there was nothing to lose, so I signed up and sent in the registration fee.

At the end of the three-day workshop, the last assignment was to write a dialogue between ourselves and someone we admired—living or dead. We were to ask this person a question that was important to us. We were free to ask any prominent historical figure: Abraham Lincoln, Martin Luther King Jr., Margaret Thatcher, or Indira Gandhi. Or we could choose some person unknown to history, who was very significant in our lives.

Instinctively, I knew I had to talk to my grandfather, and I knew exactly the question I needed to ask.

After a long period of silent meditation, I took a yellow legal pad and initiated a conversation with my grandfather. At the time, I didn't believe anything unusual would happen. I was sure that I was just going to be talking to myself on paper.

But knowing Grandpa, I should have been expecting the extra-ordinary.

Not knowing what would come next, I started writing: "Hi, Grandpa. I was hoping to have a talk with you."

After I wrote this awkward first sentence on the yellow pad, I waited. I emptied my mind of all distractions and tried to be receptive to what Grandpa might say to me. I was alone in the empty silence.

Then, from out of nowhere, a thought that was not my own came to mind. I wrote it on the pad. When I reread the sentence, I realized that Grandpa may have answered me. I felt myself mysteriously in his presence. It was as if he had taken the pen from me and begun to write on the page in his own hand, then had given the pen back to me. It was one of the most amazing experiences of my life.

I was skeptical at first. My mind kept interrupting, telling me that this couldn't be happening. Grandpa couldn't really speak to me. Maybe my memories of him were guiding my mind. I was pretty sure that must be the case.

But Grandpa kept talking. "Billy," he said, "take up that there pen of yers and write all this down on yer paper."

Suddenly, I was writing as fast as I could. I couldn't believe this was happening. The words that appeared on the page weren't words that had come to mind the way they would have if I were writing him a letter. They came to mind, but I knew I hadn't thought them. They weren't my words.

The dialogue went on for pages, my pen speeding along in spontaneous motion, scarcely stopping for punctuation, pouring ink onto the page, forming words and thoughts I would never have thought of myself. I was having a living conversation with my grandfather three years after his death. He was talking to me patiently and lovingly, and my tears were beginning to fall on the page as I wrote it all down for him.

He responded to every question, even the big one. In those incredible moments, he was alive for me. In some ways, he was more alive than at any moment I had known him in this life. I can't explain it. I'm not even going to try. He was with me. I don't know how; he just was.

I am not prepared to share very much of that conversation, but he talked to me about my questions, and that was all that mattered.

I began by telling him how confused I was that he and Grandma had lived on the same 140-acre farm for over seventy years, and that in all those years, they had never traveled more than fifty miles from the place where he was born—well, maybe once or twice. And, here I was, so dissatisfied, moving hundreds of miles every three or four years trying to find myself.

He answered me again. It was all very strange—and yet, it felt surprisingly natural.

I told him how important the stories from my childhood on the farm had been to me over the years. About how crystal-clear they had remained in my memory, and how they often preoccupied my thoughts and made me feel happy and brought a smile to my face. He didn't say anything, but I sensed that he was pleased.

As I settled into this strange dialogue, I began trying to figure out how to tell him what was bothering me. I was building up to the Big Question. I told him that I couldn't understand how he always seemed at peace with himself, so absolutely content with his life's work, not needing anything more out of life than life had given him. I desperately wanted that contentment.

"Grandpa," I asked, "how is it that you were able to stay in one place for so long and never doubt yourself, or think of leaving, or become discontent with your life?"

That was my Big Question—the question I had been waiting for years to ask, but had been too young to put into words.

"Grandpa, did you know that when I was on the farm all those years, I was bored? I hated not having anything to do. Did you know that?"

"Yep," he said, "I knew." And he picked it up. "Billy," he was still calling me by my childhood name. "Why d'you think you felt so bored on the farm?"

"I don't know, Grandpa. It's just that nothing important ever seemed to happen on the farm. It was the same thing day after day. Every morning when I woke, I wanted to go to town where there was more going on; maybe to walk down the street and get some ice cream, or buy some baseball cards, or just walk through the grocery store." I couldn't believe that I'd just told him that I was so bored on the farm that even going to the grocery store was an adventure for me. I moved on. "But Grandpa, here's what I don't understand."

"What's that?" he said.

"Now that I'm a grown man and all of that's just a memory, I long to be back on the farm more than anything. I don't really miss all those busy things we did in town. I just miss the farm. Those were the best times, and I really miss them," I repeated.

"Strange, isn't it?" he said.

"It is," I said. "I can still smell the farm, and the smell takes me right back to that place. I can hear the crunch of the crushed rock on the roadway as we walked down to the spring. Grandpa, I can feel the sheets on Grandma's bed and how good it felt to fall asleep watching the dancing shadows of the fire on the old flowered wallpaper as the kindling in the stone fireplace crackled, spat, and spewed. I can still feel it all, and I miss it so much. Grandpa, I really want to go home."

"Home feels that way, don't it?" he said.

"Yes, it does." And for the first time, I realized that this feeling I had was a feeling about home.

"Today, I'm sitting in this journaling workshop, talking to you, and this afternoon, when the boys get out of school, I want to take Jonathan and Matthew hiking in the Blue Ridge Mountains. I hope we can do some rock climbing and take some photos of the endangered peregrine falcons. Perhaps there will still be some wild blueberries in "Big Meadows." We'll stay up on the mountain until the stars come out. In the car on the way home we can listen to the Atlanta Braves baseball game on the radio, and stop at Burger King for a late dinner. It's going to be great fun.

"Hey, Grandpa, would you like to come with us?" I wrote.

"Naw," he wrote on the next line of the pad. "Y'all go on and have a good time. You need t' spend some special time with yer sons."

"But that's just it, Grandpa. We'll do all these things today, but tomorrow, I'll be back at work, feeling unhappy with my life. I don't understand." I quickly changed pens. The ballpoint

I was using was running out of ink fast, and I didn't want to miss a word of this once-in-a-lifetime talk. "How did you and Grandma have such a happy life, day after day, for over seventy years on the farm with nothing to do?"

"Well, first of all, Billy, we had plenty t' do. And second, there were a lotta happy days fer yer grandma and me there in Rock Spring, but not every day was a happy day. And third, the farm's where we belonged. That was our home. That's where we lived."

"Yes, but Grandpa, you could have gotten someone to watch the farm for a few days, and you and Grandma could have gotten on a plane and come to Washington. I would've loved to have shown you the Lincoln Memorial, and taken you to the museums, and shown you the original Constitution of the United States, and visited the White House."

"Aw," he wrote, "we didn't need t' do all those things. Like I said, we lived there on the farm."

I caught the emphasis he put on the word "lived," and made a small note in the margin to go back and think about the way he had phrased it: "… we lived there on the farm." Something about that word, "lived", and the way he put it was important. I knew it. I think he must have thought I wasn't really living.

"That's what I mean, Grandpa," I said. "I don't feel like I'm alive or really living anywhere, and I'm always wondering if I should move on to something else or be somewhere else."

"Oh, you're alive; you're just not livin' in the place where you're alive," he wrote (or I wrote for him; whichever).

"Billy, yer problem is that yer world's too big, too busy. You care right much 'bout a whole lotta things with part of yer heart, but you're missin' the one thing you need t' care 'bout with all yer heart."

"What thing, Grandpa?"

"D'you remember on the farm, how we weren't distracted by a whole lotta things? When we went t' shearin' the sheep, we just sheared the sheep. When we slopped the hogs, we were just sloppin' the hogs. When we milked the Guernsey, we were just milkin' the Guernsey, nothin' else. We were fully alive, bein' just who we were, and doin' just what the Good Lord be givin' us t' do. Nothin' more."

"Yes, Grandpa, I remember, but I still don't understand."

"Well, here it is, so write this down."

"Billy, you need t' be fully alive right where you be, just bein' exactly who yer meant t' be, just takin' care of the work the Good Lord be givin' you t' do in that place. Nothin' more. Just be alive every day, and be plowin' the fields the Lord has given you t' plow. That's how you make a home worth comin' home t'. Will you be thinkin' 'bout that?" he said.

I liked the way he put that: how you make a home worth comin' home t'. "Yes, Grandpa, I will."

I guess I hadn't realized it, but Grandpa was right. What I really wanted was a home worth coming home to. I wanted to live fully in the place where I was; to be there, and not have anywhere else I thought I needed to be, or anything else I thought I wanted to do.

"Grandpa, I want my boys to feel as good about coming home as I felt about coming to the farm. I want them to have a belonging-place that's real for them, warm with memories."

"Well, if'n that's what you really want, then best be gettin' on with it," he wrote.

"How's Carolyn?" he asked—referring to my wife, whom he had met several times before his death. She had loved my grandpa too, and he'd loved her.

"Oh, she's fine."

"Maybe," he said, "but she'd be a part of what makes yer home a home worth comin' home t'. Take good care of her."

"Okay, Grandpa. I will." I knew that I needed to share all this with her as soon as I could.

Suddenly, he grabbed the pen back from me. For some reason, he felt that he needed to get one last part down on the page. "And Billy, remember what that fossil said? Once you have a livin' place, you'll be surprised t' find that the most excitin' things you could ever experience are happenin' right there under yer feet. You don't need t' be lookin' anywhere else."

As suddenly as it had begun, the vibrant dialog began to fade. My mind began to fill up with my own thoughts. Before it was over, I quickly wrote, "Thanks, Grandpa."

And he was gone.

After that, my quest was largely over. Of course, many issues remain unresolved in my life. I still worry about them from time to time. But, after that day at the journal workshop when I decided to just "live my life," I stayed in the parish ministry for the next thirty-eight years, twenty-four of them at one church— the church that commissioned these stories. We have lived in one house for over thirty years now, and today, I hope that my boys feel that our house is a sacred place for them. I hope that they feel like it's their home.

After that day, I became, for the most part, content with my life. And to my surprise, after I finally retired from my ministry in the parish, the career I always felt unsuited to, I truly missed the people.

Sometimes, often on occasions when I least expect it, I still dig up one of those "dinosaur in the cornfield" sayings. I don't really understand where they come from. They just show up. Those old wisdom sayings might seem extinct these days, but they are found in ordinary places, so they don't get much attention. Distractions pile up so quickly, and everyday jobs require so much multitasking, that simple truths have a hard time finding their way from deep within to the surface. They remain buried under the fast pace of living, and under ways of thinking that seem new, but really aren't.

But, when in my memory I go back to simpler times, these wisdom sayings seem to walk hand in hand with my grandfather. And, as I listen, they begin to speak with one voice.

"Live your life," they seem to say. "Find what's best in you, and be who you are."

Over the years, all the stories I remember have gathered themselves together and spoken to me with one voice. They're all about my one Big Question: "How do you become content with your life, right where you are?"

I've kept that old yellow pad with the notes I made that day in the journal workshop. I get damp in the eyes every time I read them. Sometimes I wonder to myself: did it really happen?

Then I think of all that's happened since, of the gathering contentment that began to settle my heart on that magical day when Grandpa and I had our last talk. And, as strange as it sounds to hear myself say it, it really happened.

But, Grandpa always said it best...

> *"If'n you want t' be content with yer life, you need t' pour a heap of livin' into belongin' t' the place where you are, and set aside the desire t' be someplace you aren't. If'n you believe that the most excitin' things in life are buried right under yer own two feet, right where you are, then there'd be no place on this here Earth where you can go and be any happier'n you can be, bein' right where you are."*

Now, It's Your Turn:

Acknowledgements

Without the encouragement of the following people, this book would never have found its way to print. I extend my deepest thanks:

To my wife, Carolyn, who first encouraged me to write down these stories. The hours she spent proofreading and offering suggestions to strengthen the text were an immense help. Her passion helped bring *Dinosaurs* to life, and her continual encouragement and patience gave me the strength to keep on keeping on.

To my father, Dr. W. Barker Hardison, for the long hours he spent with me reviewing the stories for accuracy and helping me capture life on the farm and the dialect of the area. He could well be this books coauthor, and I greatly value his encouragement and contribution.

To Brandylane Publishers, Inc. and publisher Robert Pruett, for taking a chance on a first-time author. And to Erin Harpst, my editor, whose tireless efforts helped shape these stories into a real book. In the end, I believe she loved Grandpa almost as much as I did. And to Michael Hardison (no relation), who did the work of a graphic artist inside and out. I owe *Dinosaurs'* appealing visual layout to him. Erin and Michael's clear vision for the book helped combine its many parts into one artistic whole. Many thanks go to Grace Ball and Christina Kann, for the long hours spent proofing the final text and attending to "loose ends" too numerous to name.

Acknowledgements, *cont.*

To Candice Smith, my enthusiastic illustrator, whose unique artistic gifts add life and whimsy to the book.

To Carol Turner, Monica White, and Randy Bassett, for their support and constant encouragement. They never gave up believing that others should have the opportunity to meet Grandpa.

To my brother, Rick, who lived these stories with me and understands better than anyone how unique a man our Grandfather was.

My deepest thanks to you all.

About the Author

William Hardison is a retired minister and former adjunct professor of Christian Spirituality at Baptist Theological Seminary in Richmond. Known for his gift of vivid storytelling, he is a member of the National Storytelling Network. Dr. Hardison is a contributor to Character.org, a nationwide movement bringing fresh attention to the development of character in the lives of children through education. *Dinosaurs in the Cornfield* is his first book and deals with the development of positive character traits learned through the telling of legacy stories. He lives in Richmond, Virginia with his wife, Carolyn.

Visit the author on his website: www.williambhardisonjr.com

About the Illustrator

Candice Smith is a self-taught artist based out of Hanover County, Virginia. A mom of three girls, she is inspired by her daughters and by nature. View more of her artwork on Instagram, @domenico.art